Dave Cooke started life as a session musician on guitar and keyboards and has become a successful and award winning Media Composer and Producer. He runs his own recording studio in Twickenham producing many fine scores, songs and invoices. For more information go to www.davecooke.com

Iain Dunn is a Cambridge graduate with thirty years' experience in music, films, radio, advertising and branding. He was an award-winning copywriter and Creative Director at a clutch of leading ad agencies, helped build a radio commercials production company, was Director of Strategy at a brand agency, and now runs his own consultancy: Dunn & Co – Brand Outfitters. Iain is a member of D&AD and a deserter from the Brazilian army.

ISBN: 978-1-905665-47-1

All rights reserved. No part of this publication may be reproduced, stored in or introduced into a retrieval system, dishwasher, oven or any other cooking appliance.

Furthermore it may not be transmitted via telepathy or any spiritual medium, electronic tagging, dog tagging, dogging, are also expressly forbidden. This book must not be used for anything other than reading. Eating from, wiping, throwing, or propping up wobbly tables are not permitted. Giggling is seriously permitted.

This Book is sold subject to the condition that it shall not, by way of trade or otherwise, be lent, given away, bartered, burnt at the stake, dipped in acid, hung drawn and quartered, unless an invoice is initially applied, and posted using a first class stamp.

Finally you have only yourself to blame if this book gets stolen.

Not laughing at the contents herein is punishable by serious torment and further invoices, and may be liable to criminal prosecution which can and will be applied by the English legal system or Roger "The Hatchet" Dykeshaw who has just been released after 20 years. You have been warned.

Dave Cooke publishing

Acknowledgements

Dave Cooke and Iain Dunn would like to thank Bob Howard and Bob Johnstone without whom these invoices would not have been written.

Dave Cooke would like to thank:
Tim Bates, our fab agent, and all at Pollinger's for being brilliant and helping us in our hour of need

Teen who needed oxygen after reading the first draft and my Jems and Ames who will appreciate this more when you buy it and I can give them the money!

Jonathan Booth for his many encouragements and Chris Norris for his amazing publishing insight and advice.

Chris Sandford of Hobo Radio who gave us both some amazing work together.

Steve Cole and Martin Norfolk and all my chums who thought I had far too much time on my hands to write something so foolish, pointless and unprofitable. Please prove them wrong!

And finally, you, dear reader, as you flick through this book on your way to your holiday destination, or trying to find something for Christmas, a birthday, bar-mitzva, christening, funeral, or *'whatever'* occasion gift ... This is the one for you.

Iain Dunn would like to thank:
Judy, Jamie and Katherine for your support. I shall wear it always

For more unpublished invoices go to *www.invoicebook.com*
and check out *The Invoice Book Internet version* along
with a special *The Invoice Book* resource guide on
"How to Invoice for fun!" and regular updates.

More information also at www.davecooke.com

Foreword

Most people in the course of their daily lives come across frustrations born of other people's ignorance, stupidity or sheer obduracy.

A way of dealing with this first occurred to us when we worked together in a previous life – advertising. Together we produced many funny and original commercials, but along the way we sometimes encountered clients who were difficult, rude and, on one occasion, dangerously deranged. In these cases, the highlight of the job was the final invoice, the moment that made it all literally worth our while.

Indeed, invoicing became the most satisfying way of punishing the bad, the ugly and the downright offensive for their atrocities. 'Bob's your invoice!' we'd cackle as we wielded the mighty billing-pen with glee. We'd dream of a day when we would issue an invoice so large, that a great cavalcade would bear it down Wardour Street on a gold platter and deliver it to the door of the offending client …

Ripple dissolve to twenty years later when we found ourselves sitting in a railway café that resembled the gentlemen's conveniences on platform fifteen, drinking tea looking like it might belong in the urinal rather than in our mugs. Morosely we were comparing notes on the particularly dispiriting client meetings we'd both had. Then, somewhat inevitably, our train was cancelled. Who first suggested invoicing the train company for our wasted time is lost in the mists of time. But at that moment *The Invoice Book!* was born.

We realised that there are many people, organisations, clients and corporations who deserve to receive an invoice for something. There are also many who would benefit from this simple and harmless way of venting their frustration. So, in recognition of the inspirational days of 'Bob's your invoice!', we decided to create the 'everyman' characters of Bob Howard and Bob Johnstone (along with their respective families).

Working on the principle that if you can't beat 'em, bill 'em, the two Bobs sent dozens of invoices to anyone and everyone they felt deserved to get one. Invoices were also raised against a whole range of unsolicited suggestions for services, products and inventions.

Some replies we received were curt; a few were angry. But from a surprising number we received courteous, well-argued and even jolly letters back, many of which are reprinted here. Others simply tried to ignore us, hoping we'd go away. But we persisted, sending out reminders, and then reminders about the reminders, until we got a reply, thereby removing the corporate mask that so many companies hide behind.

Hardly any paid up, but for the one or two who did we had already decided that any proceeds from the invoices and a proportion of the book's profits would be given to charity. After all, sending the invoice and getting the response is recompense enough.

Astonishingly, the first publisher we offered the book to – Virgin Books – more or less snatched our hands off for it. They were desperate for us to finish it up.

They commissioned the cover, they edited the text, they announced a Spring launch, they issued a PR release. Then their lawyers stepped in. And suddenly we were out on our ear. Needless to say, we weren't bitter. We simply sent them an invoice. The reply was a tad frosty. After that, of course, nobody wanted to know. Not even our agent.

Salvation appeared in the form of Tim Bates. He listened to our tale of woe. He laughed at most of the letters, and chucked the others in the bin. With patience and good humour he guided us towards what you see before you. So if you don't like it, send him an invoice.

We were recently asked about the philosophy behind the book. Now, let's be clear, the two Bobs don't want to start a movement or anything like that. We're not advocating the invoicing equivalent of 'happy slapping'. But should you feel like getting things off your chest with a well-placed invoice, we'd like to encourage you. It does wonders for the blood pressure if not the bank balance. And you do get to correspond with some very interesting people; maybe even form some new relationships. Bob said the other week he could even envisage a day when we hear of a young couple getting married whose romance first started with an invoice. We're not claiming it's a cure for all the injustice in the world. All we're saying is if you feel hard done by, you can give as good as you get with an eye-wateringly large demand for payment.

So what if the train is late again and composed of only three coaches instead of twelve? Send them an invoice! Who cares if a retailer's non-existent customer service keeps you waiting in a queue on the phone for twenty-eight minutes listening to Vivaldi's *Four Seasons*? Let them pick the bones out of a nice juicy bill! Never mind that your football team charges you thirty quid just to get into the ground and sit on a plastic seat with no back, squashed next to a large gentleman with 'l.o.v.e' and 'h.a.t.e' on his knuckles and beer and onions on his breath – only to watch a wretched and dispiriting goalless draw in the freezing fog. 'It's an opportunity for growth' a friend of ours is fond of saying. Stuff and nonsense. It's an opportunity for invoicing!

Our advice to you and all the other Bobs out there is as simple as it's sweet: don't get mad – get invoicing!

Dave Cooke & Iain Dunn

"Cookeswithin"
99, Kerching Drive
Twickenham, Middx, UK

The Very Rev. Rowan Williams
Archbishop of Canterbury
Lambeth Palace,
London SE1 7J

24th March

Dear Archbishop,

I have been a supporter of yours for some time and have had no real problem with either your being Welsh, or involved with The Druids. My mother was Welsh so I feel a sort of strange kindred spirit.

My Vicar suggested that I write to you as he felt that you would be able to offer some wise and timely advice on this delicate and sensitive matter that has and continues to affect my active involvement in my local church.

My church is situated on a Red Route, which as you know means that no one is allowed to park in or around the red markings on the road. Believing that I am in God's plan, and doing his will in going to this church both morning and evening each Sunday, I make the decision to park outside the church asking for God's protection on my vehicle, and that nothing untoward will happen to it. Sadly, the local council, and their parking representatives do not feel the same way. I am not suggesting that they have been sent on a mission from Satan, or are in any way manifesting anything directly evil, but I have felt somewhat disappointed that each time I return to my car, I receive a hefty fine.

I have been a great believer in Tithing; As it clearly says in Leviticus: 'A tithe of everything from the land, whether grain from the soil or fruit from the trees, belongs to the LORD. (I'm sure that if they had cars in the Old Testament, these would have been mentioned too, don't you think?)

So coming back to my problem, I have decided that I can justify the £80 a week parking fines on the basis that it can count towards my Tithe or 10% of my income. But now, having attended for the last 3 years, I have run up a rather unsettling debt of £12,480 simply through parking outside the church.

I enclose an invoice for 10% of my total costs, asking if you would consider paying this, by way of your tithe to me, as I have paid to the church, and to the Parking authorities.

Yours Ecumenically,

Bob Howard

Ps. The 10% Invoice will again be tithed to the tune of £124.80, which in turn will be tithed again totalling £12.48p, and finally tithed at £1.25p.
It doesn't look so bad when you look at it like this does it?

Sales Invoice

Invoice No:
Date:
From:

Qty	Description	Amount exclusive of V.A.T. £	V.A.T. Nett £
	10% of £12,480.00p parking charges to be requested by way of a tithe.	£1,248.00p	

Mr B Howard
Cookeswithin
99 Kerching Drive
Twickenham
Middx

Mr Andrew Nunn
Lay Assistant to
The Archbishop of Canterbury

04 April

Dear Mr. Howard

The Archbishop of Canterbury has asked me to write thanking you for your 24th March letter and to reply. I was disturbed to hear that you have been persistently breaking the law by parking on a red line outside a church whilst you attended worship. The Archbishop cannot in any way condone law breaking of this sort and whilst he is course sorry that you have run up such an enormous debt he could not be seen to support your actions by contributing to the fine.

Christians have just as much a responsibility as non-Christians. Causing disruption and inconvenience by blocking the traffic to society is anti-social, and will bring the Church and the name of Our Lord Jesus Christ into disrepute.

"Cookeswithin"
99, Kerching Drive
Twickenham, Middx, UK

Mr Andrew Nunn,
Lay Assistant to The Archbishop of Canterbury
Lambeth Palace,
London SE1 7JU

10th April

Dear Mr Nunn,

Thank you very much for your letter on behalf of The Archbishop. Having re-read my original letter, and your reply, I can now see that it was wrong to break the law in such a blatant way, and then have the nerve to write to you and ask you to help financially. I heartily apologise for the errors of my ways in this matter.

I realise that my actions may well have given the church a bad name and feel now that I need to make some kind of formal act of contrition.

Do you think I will be excommunicated from the church?

I know that today there is a very special marriage taking place with which you, the Archbishop and all the staff at Lambeth Palace are preoccupied, but I was reading in the paper that Prince Charles and Queen Camilla are going to confess that they *"repent of and bewail their manifold sins and wickedness"*. I feel that I should do the same thing, don't you?

Do you think that the Archbishop would take me through a similar ceremony?

With regard to the original invoice I sent you, I would be happy to work off this large bill in some form of penance. Please let me know if anything springs to mind that you feel would be appropriate.

I look forward to hearing from you soon.

Yours apologetically

Bob Howard

B. Howard

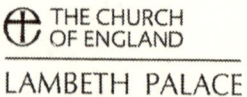

Mr B Howard
Cookeswithin
99 Kerching Drive
Twickenham
Middx

Mr Andrew Nunn
Lay Assistant to
The Archbishop of Canterbury

21 April

Dear Mr. Howard

Thank you for your 10th April letter and for your expression of regret for your actions.

The person most immediately affected by you parking on a red route while attending church (other than those road users inconvenienced by your action) was the priest of the church you attended. It is I think to him or her that you should apologise in the first instance and discuss the extent to which a formal confession and absolution are necessary. My suggestion therefore is that you discuss the matter with your parish priest.

With very best wishes

Lambeth Palace, London SE1 7JU

"Cookeswithin"
99, Kerching Drive
Twickenham, Middx, UK

Mr Andrew Nunn,
Lay Assistant to The Archbishop of Canterbury
Lambeth Palace,
London SE1 7JU

9th May

Dear Mr Nunn,

Thank you very much for your reply dated 21st April.

I am currently writing this letter to you, 56,000 feet up in the air somewhere over the Atlantic Ocean. I am returning from America where I embarked on a mission to seek out my parish priest who was taking a three-month sabbatical. It was his idea to write to you in the first place so I thought it only right to keep him up to date with my progress.

My search took me south to Palm Springs, then to San Diego, Los Angeles, through Santa Barbara and finally up to a small town called Gorda. Apart from the rather eerie feeling that everyone there was somehow related, I managed to talk to Bob, the gas station attendant, who remembered seeing my elusive reverend only a matter of hours previously. It seemed that every time I got close, he was one step ahead of me.

Sadly I never managed to meet him. However, this story does have a very happy ending. On my return trip, I stopped at a small "Danish-inspired" town called Solvang. Parking my car, this time carefully you will be relieved to hear, I walked in to one of the many souvenir shops and it was there our eyes met.

Flørnehilda was serving behind the counter selling model Viking dolls and tins of green pea soup (a town speciality so I've been told) and we immediately clicked. And now, sitting next to me on the plane home is my fiancé Flørnehilda, soon to become my bride. So I now have someone to whom I can confess and share my specific problems, even though my quest to seek out my parish priest was in vain.

I hope that you can show this letter to the Archbishop, and that he may be able to send us a personal greeting of congratulations. He wouldn't be free to take our wedding would he by any chance? We would fit around his diary if there were any chance of this happening. I thought it was worth asking just in case?

Let me know about the Archbishop's availability and I would also like to offer an invitation to you and your family to my wedding for being so kind and thoughtful with your replies. Once we have a date we can go from there.

Yours most sincerely

Bob Howard

Bob Howard and the soon to be Mrs Flørnehilda Howard

LAMBETH PALACE

Mr B Howard
Cookeswithin
99 Kerching Drive
Twickenham
Middx

Mr Andrew Nunn
Lay Assistant to
The Archbishop of Canterbury

17 May

Dear Mr. Howard

Thank you for your 9th May letter written while you were returning from the USA. Congratulations on finding so suddenly and so unexpectedly your fiancée. I hope you will be very happy together. Unfortunately the Archbishop will be unable to solemnise your marriage. I hope you understand that his diary is very congested and pleasure must take second place to duty.

With very best wishes,

Yours sincerely,

Lambeth Palace, London SE1 7JU

"TREETOPS", 58 SPITFIRE CLOSE, SOUTH CROYDON, SURREY

RSPB
The Lodge
Sandy
Bedfordshire
SG19 2DL

Dear Sirs

I am writing to you with a very sad story. Whether this is coincidence or not, last Wednesday evening I was watching "The Birds" by Alfred Hitchcock on television with my marmalade cat Boris. It is, of course, not only a classic chiller, but also a stark warning about the grave danger we all face on a daily basis. Thankfully Boris didn't seem too affected by it. Having brought a fledgling he'd dispatched earlier for my inspection, he sat contentedly on my lap throughout the film.

The morning, however, was a very different story. When I let him out to do his business in the neighbour's garden, he didn't want to go and was quite agitated. However, using the fledgling as bait, I was able to tempt him outside.

That's when I saw them.

Sitting on the wall where I normally leave bread and water out for the squirrels was a long line of menacing birds. I counted two fat Pigeons, a pair of nasty Magpies, a whole host of vicious Blue Tits, one of those vile Blackbirds, a member of the aptly-named Thrush genus and a couple of particularly evil-looking Robins. There were a number of other very threatening birds in the trees which I could not identify, but which my wife Deirdre warned me were a gang of dangerous Black Caps and Wrens.

As you can imagine, I took to my heels and raced back indoors, my heart pounding. But tragically – and here's the awful part – it was too late for Boris. Seeing those loathsome creatures and realising they had seen him must have been just too much for his little heart. With a strangled mew, his body became completely rigid. He had literally died of fright. What made it worse were the piercing shrieks of triumph those wretched birds let out before flapping away to terrorize some other poor pussycat.

Clearly it will take time for Deirdre and I to recover, but for poor, dear Boris there is no recovery. I feel strongly that as the organisation chiefly responsible for encouraging these ghastly creatures you bear the brunt of the blame and therefore the cost. I therefore enclose an invoice to cover costs and as recompense for your shocking irresponsibility.

I would appreciate prompt payment.

Bob Johnstone

Bob Johnstone

Sales Invoice

Invoice No: BOB 012

Date: _____

From: "Treetops" Spitfire Close, South Croydon

Qty	Description	Amount exclusive of V.A.T. £	V.A.T. Net £
	Sleeping pills (herbal) during post-traumatic stress period	£9.50	
	Sundry anti-bird devices to protect the garden, Including traps and anti-climb paint	£25.00	
	Punitive damages in respect of the murder of Boris And the appalling toll on Deirdre's health	£100.00	
	Cheques payable to Bob Johnstone		
		Sub total exc. V.A.T. £	
		V.A.T. £	
		Total due £	£134.50

V.A.T. rate.............................

Payment terms.....................

Tax Point ....

for birds
for people
for ever

UK Headquarters
The Lodge, Sandy
Bedfordshire SG19 2DL
Tel: 01767 680551
Fax: 01767 692365
DX 47804 SANDY
www.rspb.org.uk

Mr B Johnstone
'Treetops'
58 Spitfire Close
South Croydon, Surrey

26 May

Dear Mr Johnstone,

Thank you for taking the time to write to us about the demise of poor old Boris.

Firstly, I am sorry we have not replied to your initial letter. You may well have a point; perhaps the thieving magpies may have carried out an overnight raid on the post room in their desperate search for goodies. Not finding anything worth stealing, they took your letter out of spite.

Now what can I say about Boris! On the one hand, I can share your grief in the loss of a much loved and treasured pet, yet on the other hand and by your own admission, a prolific mouser and killer of fledgling birds had finally met his match.

Although we are Europe's largest environmental conservation charity, we are still a charity and have to account for every penny of our income. Do we ask for compensation from cat owners for the estimated 55 million birds killed each year by these opportunistic hunters? No, we do not! Let us not forget to mention the innocent by-standers traumatised by the aftermath of the carnage and the massive clean-up operation. I could also put you in contact with local vets and the RSPCA who must care for and re-habilitate these poor defenceless victims back to full health after these savage attacks.

Which is why I can only offer my heart felt condolences to you and your wife and decline to offer any monetary re-numeration.

Yours sincerely

Mike Pinhorn

Michael Pinhorn
Wildlife Adviser

"Cookeswithin"
99, Kerching Drive
Twickenham, Middx, UK

Customer Services
Nike UK Ltd.
1, Victory Way,
Doxford International Business Park
Sunderland SR3 3XF
Tyne & Wear

29th May

Dear Sir or Madam,

I have been successful in getting a place in next year's London Marathon. "*Well done!*" I can almost hear you cry. It has taken me several years to get this far and as I am not in the "first flush of youth", I am still working up to the full 26 miles required to finish this marathon Marathon. So far I am up to just over two miles, but I am very confident.

My good lady wife, by way of a gift, has decided to buy me a special costume which includes a full Nike track suit, Nike running shoes, sweat shirt, water bottle, socks, Nike hat, and a small portable oxygen tank, emblazoned, of course, with your famous Nike logo, in case of emergencies en route.

I intend to complete the course, and will be training every day both in my local park (which isn't very big but is better than nothing, especially if you run around the swings) and in my living room with improvised weights for additional strength-building (a few books, a three-legged stool, and a cast iron sewing machine). But no matter how I progress in my preparation, my trainer (the wife) and I believe that realistically, I should easily run, walk or stagger, the final distance in excess of 37 hours. This would put me in the last to complete section as you can now begin to imagine.

So I am thinking that I could indeed offer you a great service. Being one of the last, I would obviously attract specific media attention, and in so doing could offer Nike a perfect opportunity for advertising their excellent selection of products, especially on TV.

TV, and Radio advertising as you know are excessively expensive by way of their fees and I think that this presents a perfect opportunity for both parties to take advantage of this event.

To that end, I have enclosed a small, but understandably fair Invoice for my services in this area, and happy that I can help advertise your products.

Meanwhile, back to the training.

Yours in anticipation.

Bob Howard

Bob Howard

Sales Invoice

Date: _____   Invoice No: _____

From: "Cookeswithin" 99, Kerching Drive,
Twickenham, Middx, UK

Qty	Description	Amount exclusive of V.A.T. £	V.A.T. Net £
	Initial purchase at full retail price of large selection of Nike running equipment to include: Nike tracksuit, Nike running shoes, Sweatshirt, Water bottle, Socks, Nike Hat. 50% charged to Nike	£ 356.56p	
	Small portable oxygen tank with belt clip and "bullet Belt" to accommodate Extra refills.	£ 245.00p	
	Cost of Nike logo being added to Oxygen tank at Local Quick-print shop.	£ 35.00p	
	Appearance fee for end of race, and special "Last Place interview" (Wife included in fee)	£ 650.00p	
	Careful Disposal of Oxygen tank after use	£ 4.99p	
	Sub total exc. V.A.T. £		
	V.A.T. £		
	Total due £	£1,291.55p	

V.A.T. rate: _____
Payment terms: _____
Tax Point: _____

Ps. I am off to New York to see if I can get a place in their Marathon. If we can work something out, then I can take my Nike gear to America, and you know how much that could be worth don't you?

Also, I haven't approached any of your main competitors so far as I wanted to give you at Nike first option on my ideas

Our Ref. 11776/04

01/06

Dear Mr Howard

Thank you very much for your recent letter to our office requesting our support and assistance regarding next years London Marathon.

Whilst I read your letter with interest, I must stress that you are among many people who write to our organization requesting our support. As you will no doubt appreciate, we do have a limited budget for this purpose and, as such, we are not in a position to offer our support to every request we receive.

This means, unfortunately, that we are unable to help you on this occasion. I realize that this will be a disappointment to you, but I stress that Nike would like to support all deserving applications if resources permitted.

Thank you for your interest and I wish you every success in your endeavours.

Yours sincerely
for **Nike (UK) Ltd.**

Consumer Affairs Department

"Cookeswithin"
99, Kerching Drive
Twickenham, Middx, UK

Consumer Affairs Department
Nike UK Ltd.
1, Victory Way,
Doxford International Business Park
Sunderland SR3 3XF
Tyne & Wear

15th June

Dear Consumer Affairs Department,

Thank you for your letter dated 1st June. I am of course disappointed to learn of your decision not to help with my Marathon exploits for next year, but I thought it was worth mentioning something that has happened recently that may well change your mind.

Robert Johnson who is a distant cousin to Kim "Kipper" Johnson Vice President, Broadcast Operations of KBD 12 TV Station, has approached me to see if I would be interested in his new film.

Robert is currently putting together a proposal and treatment for a special Marathon programme called *The Man who came in last*.

This programme would feature my training, running around the park, working out with my weights, talking about diet and generally preparing for next year's run. Obviously due to the title of the film, I would be committed to coming in last, which I don't think will be too difficult under the circumstances. But nevertheless, planning is of the essence, and so I am asking you to reconsider your decision about your support in my using Nike sportswear and accessories.

This is a unique situation, and there's talk of doing the same thing in New York.

I would not want to dismiss your sponsorship due to a lack of interest on your part, and have to ask Adidas or Puma to take over where we left off. So I ask you to reconsider and trust that we can share the spoils of a successful relationship and appear together on TV.

Yours sincerely

Bob Howard

Bob Howard

Our Ref. 11776/04

16/06

Dear Mr Howard

Thank you very much for your further letter regarding your part in next year's London marathon.

As previously advised we do have a limited budget for any sponsorship and unfortunately we are unable to extend our commitments on this occasion.

We do sincerely aplogise that we are unable to assist you on this occasion and we do wish you every success in you training for and completion of the London Marathon. Please find enclosed a few Nike items with our goodwill.

Yours sincerely
for **Nike (UK) Ltd.**

Natalie Tite
Consumer Liaison Assistant

"Cookeswithin"
99, Kerching Drive
Twickenham, Middx, UK

Natalie Tite,
Customer Liaison Assistant
Nike UK Ltd.
1, Victory Way,
Doxford International Business Park
Sunderland SR3 3XF
Tyne & Wear

21st June

Dear Natalie,

Thank you so much for your amazingly swift reply dated 16th June. I had just come in from my daily routine around Marble Hill Park, somewhat short of puff and in need of a serious rub down with a moist flannel.

The doorbell rang and I braced myself for a weekend onslaught of Jehovah Witnesses or unwelcome boys with cheap tea towels, when my wife shouted out: "Bob, you have a parcel!"

What could it be? I wasn't expecting a delivery, as my high-density protein syringes for the over 60s had arrived two days previous.

So it was with great surprise and delight that I opened your package to find the three pairs of Nike Socks and the large Black and Red Nike water Bottle. Thank you very much! It was most welcome and will go a long way to defuse my initial disappointment with regard to our potential partnership at the next London Marathon.

I will use the socks as "lucky mascots" and rest assured that the water bottle will be full of anything that promises to get me round the course.

Any idea of what would be good? Is there a Nike Energy beverage that you could recommend? Preferably with a legal supply of speed? (Only kidding!)

Thank you again, and as you see me running at the back of the line next year I will promise to wave and acknowledge my Nike gifts from you.

Kindest regards and if I get any other bright ideas I will of course get in touch with you directly.

Yours most Victoriously,

Bob Howard

Bob Howard

"TREETOPS", 58 SPITFIRE CLOSE, SOUTH CROYDON, SURREY

Consumer Relations Dept
Cadbury Trebor Bassett
PO Box 12 Bourneville
Birmingham B30 2LU

Dear Bassetts

I am writing to you about your Licorice Allsorts, to which I am rather partial. Or at least I used to be. However I have recently encountered some disturbing fluctuations in price, size, content and quality.

First, price and size. My local corner shop seems to change its stock at random between a small bag, retailing at 89P to a slightly larger bag at 99P and then sometimes a whopper at £1.29. This is worse than checking on fluctuating petrol prices! I cannot believe that I am getting 30P worth of extra sweets for my 30P extra. And the differential between the smallest and middle-sized bags is just too small to be significant and therefore potentially very confusing - especially if I am in a hurry.

Then there's the content. Here's the big problem. Allsorts are actually limited to about 8 - 10 sorts: not 'all sorts' at all! Secondly, it seems to me that the bags are always weighted in favour of those rather nasty coconut jobbies (I suspect because they are bigger and take up more room), whereas you rarely get more than two of the delicious little blue Bertie Bassetts.

Finally, we come to quality. Here I have to give you high marks. Your product is infinitely superior to the rival upstart I was forced to buy because the retailer was not stocking yours! Superior, that is, in all but one respect: licorice. I have to say your competitor licks you when it comes to licorice, delivering a much more substantial amount of this key substance; in particular a giant all-licorice wheel which although extremely tough to chew is nevertheless the Daddy in terms of licorice content.

I hope that you will not take offence at the enclosed invoice, which I submit in order to recoup my losses when not finding a sufficient quantity of the right sort of allsorts in various sized bags purchased over the past six months. It may help to know that your remittance will of course be ploughed back into your company by continued and regular purchases of your excellent Licorice Allsorts - still excellent even if they are not the highest in licorice nor are they truly all sorts.

Yours faithfully

Bob Johnstone

Bob Johnstone

Sales Invoice

Invoice No: BOB 009

Date:
From:

Qty	Description	Amount exclusive of V.A.T. £	V.A.T. Net £
	Purchase of various bags of Bassett's Licorice Allsorts, On average 3 bags per week x 6 months (= 90 bags)	£25.80	
20	bags @ £1.29	£44.55	
45	bags @ 99P	£22.25	
25	bags @ 89P		
	Sub total	£92.60	
	Less 45% discount for allsorts I was happy with	£41.67	
	Total:	£50.93	

TREBOR BASSETT LTD

FREEPOST MID 20061
BIRMINGHAM B30 2QZ
TELEPHONE 0121 451 4432
FACSIMILE 0121 451 4435

21 April

Mr B Johnstone
'Treetops'
58 Spitfire Close
South Croydon, Surrey

Our Ref:- 1159002B

Dear Mr Johnstone,

Thank you for contacting us regarding the price of Trebor Bassett's confectionery. Currently the recommended retail selling price for Bassetts Liquorice Allsorts 180g is 99p

Since the abolition of the Retail Price Maintenance law in Great Britain, manufacturers have only been able to recommend to retailers a price at which their products should be sold. This 'Recommended Selling Price' is purely a guide and it is the decision of the stores or individual shopkeepers to decide upon a final retail selling price. Trebor Bassett do monitor the prices being charged in a very wide range of retail outlets but we can only suggest that consumers 'shop around' to achieve the best value.

With regards to your comments on the assortment of Liquorice Allsorts, the machinery used in the production of Trebor Assortments is very sophisticated, and is usually extremely accurate and reliable.

Although rare, a poor mix can result when a supply of one or more of the selection runs out and is not immediately replaced by the operator.

We would like you always to enjoy Trebor confectionery at its best. I hope you will use the attached refund for £5.00.

Thank you for taking the trouble of bringing this matter to our attention.

Yours sincerely

Helen Franklin
Consumer Relations Department

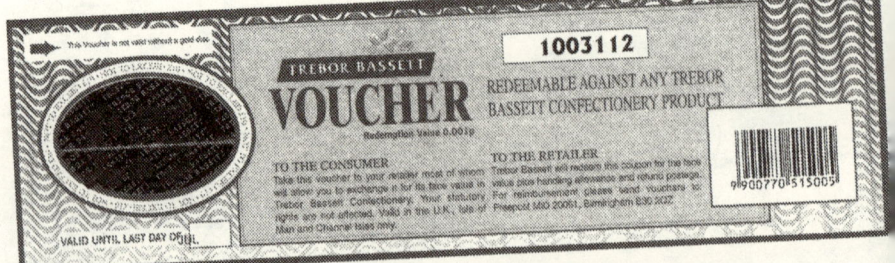

"TREETOPS", 58 SPITFIRE CLOSE, SOUTH CROYDON, SURREY

Helen Franklin
Consumer Relations Dept
Trebor Bassett
FREEPOST MID 20061
Birmingham B30 2QZ

Dear Helen

Thank you so much for your reply and gift. What truly marvellous artwork! So beautiful that I rushed out and bought a collector's display album in which to mount it. Do you have any others I could have? Or indeed could you send any other artwork relating to Liquorice Allsorts through the ages? I have decided that it would be wonderful to build up a collection of Allsorts memorabilia. To allay any fears, I enclose a signed 'guarantee' witnessed by my wife Deirdre, that the vouchers would be souvenirs only.

With regard to your comprehensive explanation of price fluctuation and suggestion that consumers 'shop around', this has given me a great idea, which I would like to share.

It seems to me that I am not alone in my love of Liquorice Allsorts and being a public-spirited sort of chap I am volunteering to start an 'Allsortswatch' service. This would monitor prices across different retailers, with a newsletter to members giving availability and prices in their area. Bertie of course would be our mascot and Deirdre has suggested the slogan "It takes Allsorts", which is jolly good, isn't it?

There are inevitably costs in getting such an ambitious project off the ground, although once we're up and running I see no reason why Deirdre and I could not run the whole thing from my son Tristan's old room. He is no longer with us. I enclose an invoice that gives you some idea of anticipated costs and would be grateful if you would get this cleared by the powers that be at your end as soon as possible so that we can crack on.

I am sure you and all at Bassett's will be as excited as I am about this idea, and I look forward enormously to hearing back from you soon.

Yours faithfully

Bob Johnstone

Bob Johnstone

P.S.
By the way, I did appreciate your kindness in not pointing out my misspelling of the word 'liquorice' in my first letter. What a mistake! Not one I shall repeat, I promise.

Sales Invoice

Invoice No: BOB 020

Date: _____

From: "Treetops" Spitfire Close, South Croydon, Surrey

Qty	Description	Amount exclusive of V.A.T. £	V.A.T. Net £
	Researching and compiling of a list of people in the Croydon area who enjoy Bassetts Liquorice Allsorts.		£95.00
	Survey of comparative prices across shops selling Liquorice Allsorts, using Deirdre and myself Employing 'mystery shopper' techniques.		£45.00
	Development of a monthly newsletter and Postage costs.		£180.00
	Construction of an "Allsortswatch.com" website To communicate with existing members and Recruit new ones.		£1500.00
	Cheques payable to Bob Johnstone		
	These costs are for covering one area only. Hopefully as things took off, we could roll it out over other areas right across the whole country!	Sub total exc. V.A.T.£	
		V.A.T.£	
		Total due£	£1820.00

V.A.T. rate...............................

Payment terms.........................

Tax Point................................

Guarantee

This is to confirm that any additional vouchers sent to Bob Johnstone at the above address will NOT be cashed in for confectionery but used simply for display purposes, and visual examples of Confectionery Artwork to accompany related promotion of "Allsortswatch" thereto.

Signed.   Witnessed by.

Bob Johnstone.   Deirdre Johnstone (wife of the Bob above)

FREEPOST MID 20061
BIRMINGHAM B30 2QZ
TELEPHONE 0121 451 4432
FACSIMILE 0121 451 4435

09 June

Mr B Johnstone
'Treetops'
58 Spitfire Close
South Croydon, Surrey

Our Ref:- 1159002C

Dear Mr Johnstone,

Thank you for your recent letter and for your idea of an "Allsorts project".

Many of the concepts including similar ideas to the one outlined in your letter have already been explored by our Research and Development Team.

We have enclosed a set of fact sheets which give information about the Trebor business, which I hope you will find interesting.

Thank you for taking the trouble to write to us and giving us the opportunity to consider your new idea.

Yours sincerely

H. Ronan.

Helen Franklin
Consumer Relations Department

"Cookeswithin"
99, Kerching Drive
Twickenham, Middx, UK

Mr R J Morris
COZENS MOXON HARTS
24 The Causeway
Teddington
TW11 0HD

3rd April

Dear Mr. Morris,

A close colleague of mine has given me your name and address, suggesting that I contact you to discuss a rather delicate and personal matter.

My wife and I have enjoyed a good income and have been fortunate to afford our two children private education.

We were also able to put our first child through University, and hope to do the same with our second daughter later this year.

As you can imagine these costs have been quite incredible, a total over 42 years of child welfare privately funded, and I have finally got to the point of asking: *"What's in it for me?"*

So the reason for my letter to you is to seek guidance and advice about the possibility of invoicing my children for services and costs.

They are both in excess of 17 years, which seems to be an age where many things are allowed. They can drink, they can get married, they can have sex (God forbid!), They can drive, and they can almost legitimately leave home with no parental permission required (Please God!).

So to that end, I have decided to draw up a detailed Invoice for the cost of each child, starting now, and see if I can claim this Invoice from Social services should neither of my children be able to pay.

It may well start them thinking that living at home isn't such a great deal after all. I will more than likely send a copy of this to Social Services to get their views, but I would value your thoughts as soon as you feel you have the time to spend on this matter. Certainly I feel that a contract would be in order, and would instruct you, on behalf of my wife and I to start drawing one up immediately.

The contract would include a clause explaining that should either or both leave home, get married, and start their own families, the costs of the invoice will be passed on to their respective main income earners.

I remain in your hands, and seek an early response.

Yours most faithfully,

Bob Howard

Bob Howard

Sales Invoice

Date: _____ Invoice No: _____

From: "Cookewithin" 99, Kerching Drive, Twickenham, Middx, UK

Qty	Description	Amount exclusive of V.A.T. £	V.A.T. Net £
	Services and costs, to include:		£160.00p
	Accommodation. Weekly charges at £80 p.w.		
	Food: Breakfast, Dinner, Snacks, Drinks, Midnight Feasts, more drinks, Wine (often stolen from cellar) Weekly charges		£160.00p
	Travel: Taxi (unofficial parental rides), Bus, Season tickets, School runs. Weekly charges		£86.00p
	Stress to parents, Worrying, Late nights, Last Minute calls, Lying awake at night, boy friends, Putting up with sullen behaviour, Grunting, Rudeness, Slamming of doors, Windows, Cupboards, Sundry Breakages. Finding and Washing of towels, Underwear, and Other unmentionables, Daily searches of rooms To find infested cups, glasses, plates, and feeding utensils, Defumigating and disinfecting, Mould removal and Emptying of bins containing Living and dead tissue. Weekly charges		£500.00p
	Telephone usage, and call charges, including Calls to Mobiles, premium line calls, Internet Downloads, Returned calls, reverse charges, Call waiting, and Texting (based on previous bill) Weekly charges		£350.00p
	Additional fees for living at home, post 18 years Using the excuse that it's cheaper, easier, better More convenient, fewer responsibilities etc. Weekly charges		£400.00p
		Sub total exc. V.A.T.£	£1746.00p
	Total per week of charges	V.A.T.£	£90,792.00p
	Total annually, paid 1st April	Total due £	

V.A.T. rate: _____

Payment terms: _____

Tax Point: _____

Cozens Moxon & Harts

SOLICITORS
COMMISSIONERS FOR OATHS

A. N. NEWMAN
* R. E. G. FARRER
* RUTH MUNBY

ASSISTANT SOLICITORS
* R. J. MORRIS · Notary Public
JANET BOND
J. KING

24 THE CAUSEWAY
TEDDINGTON
MIDDLESEX
TW11 0HD

TELEPHONE: 020-8977 4424
                       020-8977 8486

FAX: 020-8977 5116
DX 35251 TEDDINGTON

OUR REF: JK/Howard/LS

YOUR REF:

R. Howard

7th April

Dear Mr Howard,

Many thanks for your letter of 3rd April addressed to Richard Morris. Whilst Mr Morris was sad to learn of the considerable expenses you have been forced to incur in respect of your daughters, he regrets that it is not an area of law with which he is sufficiently familiar to advise you. He has, however, requested that I review your letter and provide you with a short note of advice in respect of your position.

Where monies are expended upon a family member, they are subject to the legal principle of "advancement" in the absence of an express agreement to the contrary. This principle states that the monies advanced will be treated as a gift from the benefactor to the recipient for the advancement of their life and cannot be recovered by the benefactor in the event that they come to regret the payments in question.

As you rightly state, however, your daughters are in excess of 17 years of age and as such it is open to you to place conditions upon their remaining in your property. You would only, however, be in a position to recover expenses from them in the event that they were to agree to this arrangement.

As you correctly state, Social Services will in some circumstances fund a party's housing expenses. Where, however, the Landlord is a family member the Local Authority will invariably presume that the transaction is not at arms length and, therefore, refuse to make the benefits payments in question. Indeed, many Authorities consider such claims upon them to be fraudulent.

I trust this clarifies your position.

Yours sincerely,

J. King

Jeffrey King

* Member of the Society of Trust and Estate Practitioners
* Solicitors Family Law Association Accredited Specialist

also at 35 Ashley Road, Hampton

Regulated by the Law Society

Solicitors Family
Law Association

"Cookeswithin"
99, Kerching Drive
Twickenham, Middx, UK

Mr Jeffrey King,
COZENS MOXON HARTS
24 The Causeway
Teddington
TW11 0HD

12th April

Your ref: JK/Howard/LS

Dear Mr. King,

Thank you for your letter dated 7th April, the content of which certainly does clarify my position.

I appreciate the time you have spent explaining the legality of my claim and that it isn't simply a case of sending my children an invoice.

But I did detect a note of sympathy and understanding in your letter, which I took to being subliminal agreement for the case in question.

Could this be that you already have children of your own, or perhaps thinking that this is something that is likely to happen to you in the future? My advice is "Start Saving Now!"

I may be incorrect in my assessment but, if not, do you think that I have a case to argue in presenting this claim to either the Government or even the European Parliament?

I'm certain that I could collect enough names on a petition to support a campaign called **KID** (Kid's Invoice Directive). Goodness knows that in this area alone, most children have had as much as £1,000,000 spent on them by the time they're 21 years old! I think we should do something about it before it gets completely out of control.

Do you think we have any chance of getting this through as legislation?

Not only could it solve the ever increasing problem of Children living at home until they are in their mid-thirties, it may be a more effective birth control system than those more easily available on the market.

It is very likely that you will have much more knowledge on this matter that me, so I await your judgement as to the feasibility of further action either here or in Europe.

Thank you again for your attention to this important and pressing matter and I look forward to hearing from you soon.

Yours in relative poverty,

Bob Howard

Cozens Moxon & Harts

SOLICITORS
COMMISSIONERS FOR OATHS

A. N. NEWMAN
• R. E. G. FARRER
• RUTH MUNBY

ASSISTANT SOLICITORS
• R. J. MORRIS · Notary Public
JANET BOND
J. KING

24 THE CAUSEWAY
TEDDINGTON
MIDDLESEX
TW11 0HD

TELEPHONE: 020-8977 4424
020-8977 8486

FAX: 020-8977 5116
DX 35251 TEDDINGTON

OUR REF: JK/Howard/LS
YOUR REF:

15th April

Dear Mr Howard,

Many thanks for your letter of 12th April the contents of which I note. As you will doubtless be aware, the creation of new legislation is a political process, rather than a legal one, and as such I regret that I will not be able to assist you in respect of this matter.

Yours sincerely,

Jeffrey King

• Member of the Society of Trust and Estate Practitioners
• Solicitors Family Law Association Accredited Specialist

also at 35 Ashley Road, Hampton

Regulated by the Law Society

"TREETOPS", 58 SPITFIRE CLOSE, SOUTH CROYDON, SURREY

The Managing Director
SSP
169 Euston Road
London NW1 2AE.

Dear Sir

I have written twice now to your Reef cafeteria at Waterloo Station, but as yet have not received the courtesy of a reply. I had occasion to use this establishment a while ago where I had arranged to meet a business colleague for a chat over a cup of coffee and a Danish.

I have to say there is much to commend The Reef. As well as the usual tables and chairs there are a number of comfy leatherette armchairs and even some sofas. I particularly like the feature aquarium that bisects the room. May I also congratulate your staff on serving us quickly and efficiently with splendid cappuccinos? (My pastry was a tad stale, I thought, but my colleague said his was fine.) There was however one problem which only came to light upon my return home; one which meant spending the evening in hospital.

Let me explain.

From the moment I walked through the door my wife accused me of having an affair, and I am afraid to say that your café, The Reef, is responsible. You see, because of your failure to ban smoking in your café, despite the fact that I am a non-smoker of some 20 years, my clothes reeked of tobacco. This led Deirdre to assume that I had been consorting with a floozy in some low dive. Well, one thing led to another, and when she went for me with the fish slice I jumped back, tripping over the dog, and fell awkwardly against the Formica units opening up a nasty gash in my left ear that required immediate attention. Hence having to join the ranks of the walking wounded at A&E. Happily I am now reconciled with my wife. I did this by taking her to The Reef and demonstrating the effect of your smoker-friendly atmosphere upon her own clothing.

Clearly all this has been at some considerable mental anguish and not a little cost to myself. I am therefore sending you an invoice to cover the dry cleaning bills (mine and Deirdre's), and the two coffees my wife and I had to consume during our 'experiment' (I had a cappuccino but she had a latte). I would be grateful for your cheque as soon as possible, as I am not a wealthy man and cannot fund endless cups of coffee to prove my devotion for Deirdre.

Yours truly

Bob Johnstone

Bob Johnstone

Sales Invoice

Invoice No: _BOB 001_

Date: _____

From: _"Treetops" Spitfire Close, South Croydon, Surrey_

Qty	Description	Amount exclusive of V.A.T. £	V.A.T. Net £
	Dry Cleaning:		
	1 lounge suit (grey), cream shirt and red tie (striped)	£8.99	
	1 green twin-set (wool)	£6.99	
	1 pale lilac silk blouse	£4.60	
	Refreshments at The Reef:		
	1 cappuccino (large, no chocolate)	£2.30	
	1 latte (medium)	£1.80	
	Train fares (2 off peak) Croydon to Waterloo	£10.20	
	Cheques payable to Bob Johnstone		
		Sub total exc. V.A.T. £	
		V.A.T. £	
		Total due £	£34.88

V.A.T. rate........................

Payment terms...................

Tax Point........................

SSP - creating a better experience

Select Service Partner Limited
167 Euston Road
London
NW1 2AE

Phone +44 (0)20 7543 3000
Fax   +44 (0)20 7543 2384
Web   www.ssp-intl.com

Mr Bob Johnstone
'Treetops'
58 Spitfire Close
South Croydon, Surrey

19th July

Dear Mr Johnstone

Many thanks for your letter describing your experiences both at our Waterloo Reef Cafe and subsequently in your kitchen.

Firstly may I say that I am delighted that you and Dierdre are now happily reconciled and that there is no lasting damage to your relationship. I also hope that your left ear and the dog are both recovering.

Regarding the lack of reply form the Waterloo Reef - this is clearly not acceptable although local management have been unable to trace your letter for which I apologise.

Regarding the smell of smoke on your clothes following your visits to the Reef - we do have an air-conditioning and extract system in the Reef. We also operate smoking and non smoking areas to minimise the effects of smoke nuisance to non smokers, whilst enabling smokers to indulge their habit. Whilst these steps in the occasion of your visit were obviously ineffective, for which I apologise, I do not wish to set a precedent for reimbursing customers for dry cleaning costs given that smoking is allowed in the unit. Indeed if my wife were to learn of such a precedent she would have me writing several letters a week to the owners of various hostelries around London that I frequent from time to time.

Notwithstanding, you clearly have had a traumatic experience and in the interest of good customer relations, not to mention your relationship with Dierdre, I am please to enclose a goodwill payment of £35.00.

I very much hope that you are able to find non smoking outlets in future to prevent any reoccurrence of this most regrettable occurrence

Yours sincerely

Tony Keating
Managing Director
SSP, UK Rail
Enc.

"Cookeswithin"
99, Kerching Drive
Twickenham, Middx, UK

Accounts Department
Battersea Dogs Home
4 Battersea Park Rd
Battersea
London SW8 4AA

24th March

Dear Sir/ Madam,

It is with great sadness that I write this letter to you. Some time ago, I was fortunate to find a small canine companion at your trusted establishment. It was mutual affection at first sight, so to speak.

I was diligent in preparing my home for "Scallywag's" arrival and we both settled down to what I has imagined to be many years together. Imagine my surprise when I discovered that only after a week, this poor animal had popped his paws and was no more. Happily he didn't suffer, but I now feel the great irony of what people say about pets pressing heavily on my heart, and even more distressingly, on my wallet.

"A Dog is for life".

Having thought that My dog was for life, I had been to a local pet superstore and purchased several years supply of canned food, multi-coloured dog biscuits, 45 chewy toys and 18 different clothing accessories mainly to compensate for the cold spell we've been having recently.

Knowing that your Patron: Her Majesty the Queen and your President: His Royal Highness Prince Michael of Kent would be sympathetic to my plight, I felt it only right to send with this letter, an invoice that covered the costs of everything I had purchased, excluding what was used before Scally passed away of course.

If there were any chance of recompense, I would gladly donate the remaining surplus to one of your many fine establishments. I look forward to hearing from you in due course.

Yours sadly,

Bob Howard

Bob Howard

Sales Invoice

Date: _____ Invoice No: _____
From: _____

Qty	Description	Amount exclusive of V.A.T £	V.A.T. Net £
476	cans of Chum (Large size) with extra rabbit	£252.99p	
165	jumbo sacks of mixed dog biscuits	£152.76p	
44	chewy toys (one was slightly chewed!)	£87.12p	
17	doggy coats, and other clothes (I buried him in one of the outfits (it only seemed right)	£127.98p	
	Total	£622.85p	

Battersea Dogs Home
Patron: Her Majesty The Queen
President: His Royal Highness Prince Michael of Kent

4, Battersea Park Road, London SW8 4AA
Tel: 020-7622 3626   Fax: 020-7622 6451
www.dogshome.org

Mr Bob Howard
Cookeswithin
99 Kerching Drive
Twickenham
Middx

12 May

Dear Mr. Howard

Thank you for your letters of 24 March and 12 April respectively and please accept my apologies for the delay in replying.

I am sorry to hear of the loss of your dog Scallywag and our sympathies are with you.

Unfortunately we have no record of you rehoming a dog from us. Your name or address does not appear in our rehoming system and there is no paperwork.

Even if we did have, it is not our policy to refund purchases of pet items unless they are from our own shop and are faulty. I would suggest that you approach the pet superstore you purchased them from and explain the circumstances.

I am very sorry to be the bearer of bad news and once again please accept our condolences on your loss.

Yours sincerely,

David Newall
Director of Administration
Direct line: 020 7627 9204
E-mail: d.newall@dogshome.org

Battersea Dogs Home
4, Battersea Park Road,
London SW8 4AA
Tel: 020-7622 3626
Fax: 020-7622 6451

Battersea at Old Windsor
Priest Hill, Old Windsor,
Berkshire SL4 2JN
Tel: 01784 432929
Fax: 01784 471530

Battersea at Brands Hatch
Crowhurst Lane, Ash,
Kent TN15 7HH
Tel: 01474 874994
Fax: 01474 872855

A Member of The Association of Dogs and Cats Homes
Company Limited by Guarantee. Registered in England No. 278802   Registered as a Charity under the Charities Act 1960 No. 206394
VAT Registration No. 726 5204 47 Registered Office: Battersea Dogs and Cats Home, 4 Battersea Park Road, London SW8 4AA

"Cookeswithin"
99, Kerching Drive
Twickenham, Middx, UK

David Newall,
Director of Administration
Battersea Dogs Home
4 Battersea Park Rd
Battersea
London SW8 4AA

17th May

Dear David,

Thank you at last for your reply, and your condolences. I appreciate your predicament regarding my mountain of merchandise. First of all, I think I can shed some light on the paperwork conundrum.

A week before Scallywag's departure, I was sitting comfortably listening to *The Archers*, with a glass of sweet Amontillado, when I heard a knock at the front door. I opened it and saw a smartly dressed man, holding a dog. He claimed to be from your dog's home and showed me a document, which I now understand, was a fake. I was taken in by the dog, and the man's story. He claimed to be doing a *"Door-to-door' – Battersea dog's home public relations exercise* in an attempt to recruit new customers. He claimed that a previous owner had mishandled *Bruiser* and would I take him in for a short while. Of course I agreed, not really thinking that I needed to sign anything, or ask for any official paperwork. I had just finished with my long-term boyfriend, Tarquin, and I was feeling a little "washed up like a deflated lilo at low tide". So I took one look at Bruiser, and he at me, and after I'd decided to rename him Scallywag (Bruiser being such an ugly name), I paid the man £126 and took my new friend in. Little did I realize the trouble It would cause.

Secondly, I have had an idea that may well solve the problem with my unwanted canine commodities. Could I use your name to advertise a local Car Boot Sale, or maybe I should call it a Dog Kennel Sale? Then maybe I could attract other dog owners who would like to purchase some of the food, and toys, and your name would add credibility to my story.

I love the three-dog logo at the top of your paper; if you could send me a few stickers I could use them in my sale.

I hope that this clears up the mystery and that we can bring this sorry tale (no pun intended!) to a happy-ish ending.

I await your comments, and hopefully, stickers, and I'll let you know when I'm doing the sale, and perhaps you could come over for a sherry?

Thank you again for your valuable time in replying and I look forward to hearing from you soon.

Sincerely

Bob Howard

Bob Howard

Battersea Dogs Home
Patron: Her Majesty The Queen
President: His Royal Highness Prince Michael of Kent

4, Battersea Park Road, London SW8 4AA
Tel: 020-7622 3626   Fax: 020-7622 6451
www.dogshome.org

Mr Bob Howard
Cookeswithin
99 Kerching Drive
Twickenham
Middx

23 May

Dear Mr Howard,

Thank you for your reply of 17 May. The way that you came about owning "Scallywag" sounds very interesting, but it does concern us that someone is going door-to-door claiming to be from Battersea Dogs Home public relations department. For your future information, we do not ever send people out door-to-door.

Your idea of having a car boot sale is a good one, however, we are unable to allow you to use our name or logo. It is only used in events that we sponsor.

We wish you luck in selling your canine items and for your reading pleasure, I enclose the latest copy of our PAWS magazine.

Yours sincerely,

David Newall
Director of Administration
Direct line: 020 7627 9204
E-mail: d.newall@dogshome.org

Battersea Dogs Home
4, Battersea Park Road,
London SW8 4AA
Tel: 020-7622 3626
Fax: 020-7622 6451

A Member
Company Limited by Guarantee. Registered in Engla
VAT Registration No. 726 3204 47 Registered C

paws
Battersea Dogs Home Magazine

The best of friends
Why Greyhounds make great companions

The kitty book of calm
Helping cats to handle stress

Battersea Dogs Home

"Cookeswithin"
99, Kerching Drive
Twickenham, Middx, UK

SHELL UK.
Customer Care,
Ground Floor,
Rowlandsway House,
Rowlandsway,
Wythenshawe,
Manchester,
M22 5SB.

24th March

Dear Sir / Madam,

It has taken a little time for me to get round to writing this letter to you. I suppose I wanted to see how last week's Budget affected the increase of fuel prices, and how specific garages reacted to it. Sadly Shell didn't come out too well and my complaint is one that I feel highlights the rather cynical and exploitative way oil companies like you deal with their customers.

The day after the March Budget (17th March), I visited my local Shell garage in Twickenham and didn't really think to check the price of fuel. I was therefore amazed to discover that in less that 24 hours after the budget had been announced, the prices had risen by a massive 4 pence per litre, to 85 pence per litre of unleaded fuel.

The day after that, the price suddenly dropped to 82 pence per litre, and then, the following Monday, the price went zooming up again to 85 pence per litre again. Yesterday (23rd March) as I was driving, I noticed another Shell garage selling for a modest 82 pence per litre. What is going on??? Have you no shame? Do you think we are all idiots??

What gives you the right to price your fuel costs on an apparent random basis, with no real regard for fair play, the law, or the drivers who pay your astronomic salaries? There is a principal at stake here, but there's also the money. I am therefore enclosing an invoice that I would kindly but firmly request you pay, to cover the difference between the costs of petrol inaccurately charged post-Budget day, and the time, inconvenience, and travel time it has taken to find a better filling station that charges a fair and accurate price for their fuel.

I trust that you will deal with this matter as quickly as you instruct your garages to put up their prices, and I look forward to a speedy and amicable response.

Yours most sincerely

Bob Howard

Sales Invoice

Invoice No:
Date:
From:

Qty	Description	Amount exclusive of V.A.T. £	V.A.T. Net £
	Price difference on 40.75 litres of fuel, originally charged at 85 pence per litre, which should have been 81 pence per litre	£1.84p	
	Time, travel, and mileage costs to find suitable Alternative garage	£6.87p	
	Additional costs and sundries, P&P.	£2.29p	
	Total payable	£11.00p	

Shell U.K. Oil Products Limited
Retail Customer Service
Rowlandsway House
Rowlandsway
Wythenshawe
Manchester
M22 5SB
Tel 0800 731 8888
Fax 0161 499 4903
Internet http://www.shell.com/uk

Mr Howard
Cookeswithin
99 Kerching Drive
Twickenham
Middx

Our ref: 18529

30th March

Dear Mr Howard

Thank you for your recent letter regarding fuel prices.

When deciding an appropriate recommended price we take a number of factors into account but the most influential is the price set by local competitors. Petrol prices are displayed very prominently and customers are well aware of them. As a result small differences in price can result in a significant swing of sales so it is not surprising that nearby service stations display the same or similar prices - they simply cannot afford to be out of line.

The aggressiveness of competition does, however, differ from place to place. This means that although prices in local areas are often very close to one another, variations can occur. The most intense competition tends to occur in areas with high population densities having a mixture of supermarkets and traditional service stations. Each service station operates within its own competitive environment, so each service station is looked at individually regarding fuel pricing, taking into account a number of different factors - different levels of competitive intensity, the proximity of competitors, traffic flows, customer base (local regular customers or transient customers), throughputs, operating costs and so on.

Shell does not adopt of a national price for fuel but fluctuates against competition in any given area. I would like to categorically reassure you that Shell UK are not profiteering at the expense of our valued customers. The UK petrol retailing industry is fiercely competitive, evident by the rapid expansion into fuel retailing by the supermarket chains and the high visibility of fuel prices on forecourt pole signs. Interestingly and as a direct result of the high levels of competition our fuel prices in the UK excluding excise duty and VAT are amongst the cheapest in the world.

Our aim is to provide customers with excellent value for money, not only as far as price is concerned but also in terms of the facilities we offer at each site, location, convenience and customer care. I can also confirm that the refining and quality testing process employed by Shell ensures that our customers receive the best quality fuel at very competitive prices.

I am unable to reimburse your enclosed invoice, however I would like to thank you for taking the time to contact Shell UK with your comments.

Yours sincerely

Heather Whyte
Customer Relations – Retail

"Cookeswithin"
99, Kerching Drive
Twickenham, Middx, UK

Heather Whyte
SHELL UK.
Customer Care,
Ground Floor,
Rowlandsway House,
Rowlandsway,
Wythenshawe,
Manchester, M22 5SB.

6th April

Your Ref: 18529

Dear Heather,

Thank you so much for your reply to my letter regarding fuel prices. I don't know how you found the time to go into such detail. I got the feeling you were explaining things very patiently to me, rather like a teacher speaking slowly and carefully to a rather dense schoolboy. I just wish I understood any of it!

The only bit I did understand was when you said you are "unable" to reimburse my enclosed invoice. But why are you unable? Please be clear that I am not expecting you to foot this bill personally. That would just be silly. So it must be Shell that is unable. But this is where I'm confused, Heather. After all, your annual profits after tax were reported as £9.2bn – a rise of 55% on last year. And yet you have to hike the prices at the pumps and you are unable to reimburse me.

So how can we work together on this? There are people out there who view such excessive profits as obscene. They use words like "corporate greed" and "profiteering". If only they knew that you are unable to pay a bill for 25 quid, they might see how strapped you are for cash.

Do you have any suggestions as to how you might be able to pay me, given time? Would it help to do it on the drip at, say, a fiver a week? Or perhaps if I were to extend interest-free credit for 6 months, would that see you out of your short-term cash-flow difficulty? Or is there any other way I can help you?

Please let me know, as I'm anxious to come to some agreement with you.

Yours hopefully

Bob Howard

Bob Howard

Shell U.K. Oil Products Limited
Retail Customer Service
Rowlandsway House
Rowlandsway
Wythenshawe
Manchester
M22 5SB
Tel 0800 731 8888
Fax 0161 499 4903
Internet http://www.shell.com/uk

Mr Howard
Cookeswithin
99 Kerching Drive
Twickenham
Middx

Our ref: 18529

7th April

Dear Mr Howard

Thank you for your recent letter dated the 6th April

I am sorry that you are dissatisfied with my response to your original letter.

As you are already aware, petrol prices are displayed very prominently and customers are well aware of them. Therefore it is the customer's choice to use a service station which offers the best value for money.

Shell does not adopt a national price for fuel but fluctuates against competition in any given area and I can assure you that the recent budget was not the reason behind recent fuel price increases at Shell service stations. Once again, I would like to categorically reassure you that Shell UK are not profiteering at the expense of our valued customers. Therefore I am unable to reimburse the costs on your invoice.

Yours sincerely

Heather Whyte
Customer Relations – Retail

"Cookeswithin"
99, Kerching Drive
Twickenham, Middx, UK

Heather Whyte
SHELL UK,
Customer Care,
Ground Floor,
Rowlandsway House,
Rowlandsway,
Wythenshawe, Manchester, M22 5SB.

10th April
Your Ref: 18529

Dear Heather,

I received your letter of 7th April, and now that you have repeated word for word some of the things you wrote in your first reply it has all suddenly come clear to me. Don't you find that sometimes? When we say the same thing twice it makes it more understandable. When we say the same thing twice it makes it more understandable. See what I mean?

Anyway I now understand (because you've said it twice) that *"Shell UK are not profiteering"* because *"Shell does not adopt a national price for fuel but fluctuates against competition in any given area."*

I also realize from both your letters that *"prices are displayed very prominently and customers are well aware of them"*. However, Heather, are they aware that *"Shell UK are not profiteering"* because *"Shell does not adopt a national price for fuel but fluctuates against competition in any given area"*? Surely in the interests of good relations with your valued customers it is vital that they do.

I am told that advertising – a bit like your letters – works by repetition. So I have prepared some adverts, which should be *"displayed very prominently"* next to your prices at every Shell station. These adverts reflect your theme that *"the UK petrol retailing industry is fiercely competitive"*, which is why I've gone for placards like: "SHELL – NOT AS MUCH A RIP OFF AS ESSO DOWN THE ROAD." or "SHELL – NOT AS BLATANT PROFITEERING AS BP" or "SHELL – NOTHING LIKE A TOTAL TUCK UP." or "SHELL'S BELLS-WHY Q8 TO PAY PRICES THAT ARE MORE EXTORTIONATE!"

I am sure you will want to use these adverts and so I have enclosed an invoice for the work involved. Like you, my aim is to provide you with excellent value for money, and I can also confirm that the quality testing process employed by me ensures that you receive the best quality adverts at very, very competitive prices.

I eagerly anticipate seeing my placards up soon at my local Shell station, and look forward to receiving payment shortly. I really hope you like them.

Yours most sincerely

Bob Howard

Sales Invoice

Invoice No: _____
Date: _____
From: _____

Qty	Description	Amount exclusive of V.A.T.E	VAT Not E
	4 original placards with creative copy	£100.00p	
	Royalty usage – for UK only	£300.00p	
	Carried forward from previous invoice	£21.00p	
	Total payable	£321.00p	

SHELL

"NOT AS MUCH A RIP OFF AS ESSO Down THE ROAD"

SHELL

"Not as Blatant Profiteering as BP"

SHELL

"NOTHING LIKE A TOTAL TUCK UP."

Shell's Bells!

"WHY Q8 TO PAY PRICES THAT ARE MORE EXTORTIONATE!"

"TREETOPS", 58 SPITFIRE CLOSE, SOUTH CROYDON, SURREY

QVC
Customer Operations Centre
South Boundary Road
Knowsley Industrial Park
Knowsley, Liverpool
L70 2QA

Dear QVC

I am a big fan of The Shopping Channel. Although there are other pretenders to the throne, there is still only one king! The others do not worship the merchandise as sincerely as you do; with reverence and a certain awe. With them there is just too much razzamatazz. I can watch for a bit but then it becomes irritating, whereas with QVC I can watch for hours. Indeed last night I was glued to your 3-hour Gem Fest. You see, we recently experienced the trauma of a burglary where my wife's jewellery was stolen and we were hoping to replace several items with some prudent purchasing on your channel.

Anyway, we were thoroughly enjoying the show, and especially the lighthearted banter between Julia Roberts and Dale Franklin, when the most extraordinary thing happened. On came a Pink Sapphire solitaire ring being modelled by the lovely Chrissie that looked exactly like the one Deirdre used to have. Next came an Amethyst and Opal cluster pendant – just like Deirdre's old one. It was not until we saw the Brazilian gem briolette cut drop earrings in Blue Topaz that we realised the truth. Not only did all this jewellery look like Deirdre's – it was Deirdre's!! We just sat there with our mouths open as item after item came on – all from Deirdre's collection.

Now, I have no idea how you came by stolen goods, and I'm sure there is a perfectly innocent explanation. Certainly I have no wish to accuse, let alone condemn. "Let he who is without sin cast the first stone" the Good Book says; "preferably a gemstone", say I!

No, my aim is much more pragmatic. You see. Deirdre feels that her precious gems were 'violated' in the robbery, and she would now feel 'soiled' wearing them even if you returned them to her. So instead, I am sending you an invoice for the value of the goods we spotted on the channel, and once we receive your remittance we will be able to put it towards a whole new jewellery collection – all bought from QVC of course! I am sure that you will agree that rather than getting into a fruitless witch hunt, this is the best way to solve a rather embarrassing matter to everyone's mutual satisfaction. We look forward to receiving payment so that Deirdre and I can spend many happy hours watching more Gem Fests, Gems Galore and Rainbow of Gems, rebuilding Deirdre's collection.

Yours very sincerely

Bob Johnstone
Bob Johnstone

Sales Invoice

Invoice No: **BOB 019**

Date: _____

From: _"Treetops" Spitfire Close, South Croydon, Surrey_____

Qty	Description	Amount exclusive of V.A.T. £	V.A.T. Net £
	Recovery of value of Deirdre's stolen jewellery collection which subsequently appeared on QVC – The Shopping Channel		
	0.32ct Opal & 0.44ct Ruby flower cluster ring 9ct gold		£39.98
	1ct Pink Sapphire solitaire style ring 9ct gold		£171.36
	0.54ct Pink Sapphire Swiss set ring 9ct gold		£76.50
	3.3ct Lima Quartz and 1ct Aquamarine 3 stone ring 9ct gold		£56.25
	2.5ct Amethyst & Opal cluster pendant & 45cm chain 9ct gold		£64.92
	Brazilian gem briolette cut drop earrings Blue Topaz 9ct gold		£43.64
	0.85ct Tanzanite graduating 5 stone ring 9ct gold		£137.25
	Emerald & Diamond accent exotic bar ring 9ct gold		£81.20
	0.88ct Brazilian Amethyst & 1.92ct Rhodolite floral ring 9ct gold		£55.00
	London Blue Topaz & Tanzanite pendant and chain 9ct gold		£77.00
	0.78ct Emerald 0.1 set Diamond band ring 9ct gold		£108.92
	0.5ct Tanzanite Pink Sapphire & 0.25 Diamond ring 9ct gold		£182.00
	Multi Gemstone cross pendant with green cord & 45cm chain		£69.98
	Cheques payable to Bob Johnstone		
		Sub total exc. V.A.T. £	
		V.A.T. £	
		Total due £	£1164.00

V.A.T. rate.............................

Payment terms.....................

Tax Point..............................

Customer Operations Centre	Telephone: 0800 514131
Liverpool	Telephone: Rep of Ireland 1-800 535949
L70 2QA	Website: www.qvcuk.com

21st April

MR B JOHNSTONE
Treetops
58 Spitfire Close
South Croydon
Surrey

Dear Mr Johnstone,

Thank you for taking the time to write to us at QVC.

I was sorry to hear about your recent burglary but I do assure you that the items you saw on air were not your property. The items shown by QVC presenters are samples of the items we sell and supplied by our carefully vetted vendors.

The studio has a sample to display on air and we have many more identical copies of the items available for sale.

If you need any further assistance please do not hesitate to contact QVC.

Yours sincerely,

Carol Sanders
Customer Service Operations

Registered Office: Marco Polo House, 346 Queenstown Road, London SW8 4NQ. Registration Number 2807164.

"TREETOPS", 58 SPITFIRE CLOSE, SOUTH CROYDON, SURREY

Carol Sanders
Customer Operations Centre
QVC
South Boundary Road
Knowsley Industrial Park
Knowsley, Liverpool
L70 2QA

Dear Carol

Thank you so much for your reply to my letter. How thrilled I was to get a personal note from someone in television; I feel as if I am mixing with the stars! I don't suppose you know anyone from 'Brookside', do you? I was a big fan for many years. And of course, before that, 'The Liver Birds'. I met Polly James once.

Anyway, enough of this blether, and let's get down to business.

I am very surprised that you can categorically guarantee that none of the goods appearing on your channel are stolen. For various reasons which I cannot go into, I have a number of contacts with the underworld, and only recently I was in The Blind Beggar pub in London's East End chatting to a character called Frankie 'Fingers' Bartram. He told me that Freddie the Fence had told him that television and online companies are often used as a way of 'laundering' stolen goods. In fact, Frankie and I are currently in negotiation with Channel 4 over an investigative documentary into this scam. I wonder, Carol, would you like to be in it? With your knowledge of television I am sure you would make a wonderful expert witness. Please let me know if you are interested and I will put you in touch with the producer in charge of the project.

In the meantime, if you are certain that QVC is not an unwitting accomplice in anything illegal, I have a brilliant suggestion to make. At the very least, as you demonstrate the merchandise I think you should have onscreen captions that say "These are not stolen goods". Also I could make a guest appearance to reassure people about this. I can assure you I would be very good at this, having studied the techniques of your current presenters and also having recently played a bear in my daughter's school production of 'Goldilocks'. The head teacher told me afterwards I was the best of the three by far.

Please let me know when you would like me to come and make this appearance. My fees would be quite modest since it would be such a thrill to appear on my favourite television channel.

Yours very sincerely

Bob Johnstone

Bob Johnstone.

THE SHOPPING CHANNEL

CHIEF EXECUTIVE OFFICE

16th June

Mr Bob Johnstone
Treetops
58 Spitfire Close
South Croydon
Surrey

Dear Mr Johnstone
RE: Request to appear on QVC

Thank you for your recent letter and request to appear on QVC.

After speaking with the director of production, we apologise that we cannot offer you a guest appearance on QVC at this time however, your request has been filed for future reference.

If you have any further questions regarding this matter please do not hesitate to contact myself on our free phone number 0800 51 41 31, ask for your call to be transferred to Jackie Sidekli in the Chief Executive Office. I will be happy to help.

Yours sincerely

Jackie Sidekli
Chief Executive Office

CUSTOMER OPERATIONS CENTRE
LIVERPOOL
L70 2QA
Telephone: 0151 551 2500
Facsimile: 0151 551 2585

Registered Office. Marco Polo House, Chelsea Bridge, 346 Queenstown Road, London SW8 4NQ. Registration Number 2807164.

"Cookeswithin"
99, Kerching Drive
Twickenham, Middx, UK

General Enquiries
Madame Tussauds
Marylebone Road
London

29th June

Dear Manager of Madame Tussauds,

My name is Robert Howard and I am ten years old. My dad has let me use his computer to write this letter to you. I hope you don't mind.

The thing is, I am wondering what it takes to get someone made into one of your models? I know that most people you choose are famous and on TV, but I wanted to ask you if you would do me a favour.

At School we have a great Art teacher called Mr Johnson. He is always making us laugh and drawing silly things on the blackboard especially when the headmistress isn't around. Some of his pictures are a bit naughty, but we don't tell anyone (so far).

Our class have got together and would like you to make a model of Mr Johnson so we can come to London and visit him, and laugh at him. Would you like to do this for us? He might even become famous if loads of people see him standing there in front of his blackboard.

My dad says it's a silly idea and Mr Johnson wouldn't be able to take the time off work for you to take measurements, so I have asked Mr Johnson how much he would have to charge to miss school for a day to come and see you. He says it's about £65 plus his train fare. Do you think you could pay this?

My dad says that the best way is to send in what he calls an invoice so you can see how much it costs really. I've never heard of that word but I trust my dad and he's shown me what to write.

I've put my address on this letter so you can let me know. I hope that you can do this for us: tell everybody to visit you.

Thank you

Bob Howard

Robert Howard

Sales Invoice

Invoice No:
Date:
From:

Qty	Description	Amount exclusive of V.A.T. £	V.A.T. No £
	Mr Johnson would like for one day	65.00p	
	His train fare there and back	6.00p	
Ps.	Please write back soon		

13th July

Mr Robert Howard
Cookeswithin
99 Kerching Drive
Twickenham
Middx

Dear Robert,

Thank you for your letter of 29th June. I am sorry I could not reply to you sooner.

Although we would love to make a wax figure of your art teacher Mr Johnson, regrettably, it would be too expensive. It costs anything from £60,000 upwards so we have to be very selective about who we choose to include in our attraction.

Taking the measurements does not take too long - around 2 hours - it can then take around 6 months to create the finished wax figure. We call this 'a sitting'. If you think that every single hair on the head needs to be inserted one by one and this alone take up to around 6 weeks, depending on how much hair that person has (how much hair does your teacher have??)

For those celebrities who are too busy to come to us for a sitting, we will travel around the world to go to them!

At Madame Tussauds we do run special sessions called Studio Secrets which is a show we put on for schools which runs through the history of Madame Tussauds and shows you the process for making wax figures. This has to be booked in advance. There is also the opportunity for teachers to be called up on stage to take part in the show. Perhaps you could persuade Mr Johnson to bring you and your class?

Anyway, I enclose some information for you on the wax figure making process.

Thank you very much for taking the time to write to us and I hope you will visit Madame Tussauds soon.

Kind regards,

Susanna Lamb
<u>Guest Experience</u>

"Cookeswithin"
99, Kerching Drive
Twickenham, Middx, UK

Miss Susanna Lamb
Guest Experience
Madame Tussauds
Marylebone Road
London NW1 5LR

1st August

Dear Miss Lamb,

Thank you very very much for your letter. I was very excited to get it, especially when I'd told my best friends that I had written to you and that you might be able to make a copy of Mr Johnson.

There is one peace of good news: Mr Johnson is completely bald. I think something happened to him when he was younger which left him with no hair, no eyebrows, or any hair anywhere. That's not exactly true. He has one enormous ginger hair growing out of his nose. I think he pretends it's not there but it's really hard not to stare. Would that change the cost of making him into wax? I could send you a picture of him if you like? We draw him on our books all the time.

My Dad read your letter and wanted me to ask you what they used to call you at school. They call me Howardy-Custard!

I love your name but he says that it would make some funny nicknames like "SLAMB-Dunk" which I don't understand. Did you have a favourite name?

I think I will tell Mr Johnson about the Studio Secrets and try to fix a trip sometime next term.

I hope you can write back to let me know if a picture of Mr Johnson would help.

Thank you and I hope you have a nice holiday.

Bye for now

Bob Howard

Robert Howard

10th August

Mr Robert Howard
Cookeswithin
99 Kerching Drive
Twickenham
Middx

Dear Robert,

Many thanks for your letter of 1st August

As stated in my letter to you of 13th July, regrettably, we will not be able to make a wax figure of your teacher, Mr Johnson, as it would be too expensive.

Your Dad is right, I do get called some funny names (Lamb Chop), however I have only had the name for about 9 years as I married a Lamb! (My husband had some even funnier names when he was at school!)

Hope that your Dad or your school will bring you to Madame Tussauds for a visit soon,

Regards,

Susanna Lamb
Susanna Lamb
Guest Experience

contact us
www.madame-tussauds.com
Marylebone Road London NW1 5LR Tel +44 (0)20 7487 0200 Fax +44 (0)20 7465 0862
Madame Tussauds is a division of Tussauds Attractions Limited. Registered in England No. 1284934. Registered Office: York Court, Allsop Place, London NW1 5LR
LONDON · NEW YORK · LAS VEGAS · AMSTERDAM · HONG KONG

"Cookeswithin"
99, Kerching Drive
Twickenham, Middx, UK

Dulux Customer Care Centre
ICI Paints
Wexham Road
Slough
SL2 5DS

29th May

Dear Customer Care Centre,

My name is Bob Howard and I run a successful painting and decorating company. It's small and my daughter, Hattie, is my only employee. We are busy and have many clients in the high-class areas around Richmond and Chiswick who demand a very high standard and excellent service.

I have also been a great supporter of Dulux paints for my whole professional life knowing them to be durable and reliable, whilst retaining a competitive edge price-wise. (I sound like I'm giving a speech at one of your corporate events, don't I?) Anyway, an idea has been brewing (and mixing!) for some time and I wanted to pass this by you so that we could both take advantage of it as soon as possible.

I want to patient my new brand of Paint Colours called *"Howard Hues"*. Brilliant don't you think? *"Howard Hues"* is a custom built range of new colour textures that are original and only available though me so far. I've started to mix these in my shed using several domestic blenders but now feel I need to expand into mass production. I want to offer my clients their own special kind of colours and in keeping with the area I service, they have names that they understand and relate to.

Private School – a shade of light green has proved to be a favourite, as has *Tennis Club* which is a slightly off white with a hint of blue. *Four by Four* is a darker colour with black being predominant, *Second home, in the country* boast a rather gentle shade of cream and subtle yellow. I have many other colours and I would be more than happy to send you some samples of my blends.

I have also enclosed an invoice of my new colours and hope that we can come to some mutually agreeable arrangement and very soon go into business together. I also want to paint my van with my new logo *"Howard Hues"* and Dulux. *Reassuringly expensive.*

Please let me know how we can move forward together to make this even more successful.

Kind Regards and hear from you soon.

Yours sincerely

Bob Howard
Bob Howard

Sales Invoice

Invoice No: _____
Date: _____
From: _____

Qty	Description	Amount exclusive of V.A.T. £	V.A.T. Net £
	Full range of "Howard Hues" Colour textures, including formula and labels. 26 new and original Blends	£1356.99p	
	Re-painting of Van to include Dulux Name and new logo	£124.78p	
		£1481.77p	
	Total payable		

ICI Group Intellectual Property
PO Box 1883
Wexham Road
Slough PDO
Berkshire SL2 5FD
England

Telephone (01753) 550000
Fax (01753) 877247

Your ref.	Our ref. M-260-SL (Please Quote)	Direct Dial 01753 877235	Date 28 June

Dear Mr Howard

Howard Hues paint colours

Thank you for your letters dated 29th May and 19th June, which have been passed to me today. I apologise for that our reply was delayed as your letters had been passed by the Customer Care Service through to our marketing departments to see what interest they might have in your concept.

I am sure you will understand that at any time we have a number of people working within our company on new concepts for colour themes and on new colour ranges and that from time to time we also receive similar proposals from customers, suppliers, design agencies and other interested parties.

Having checked with our innovations teams, I regret that we do not have an interest at this time in taking forward your proposal to work together on a new paint range.

We are of course delighted to hear that you are such a strong supporter of our **Dulux** paints but we cannot give our consent to your use of our **Dulux** logo on your van as our trade team is only authorised to allow our logo to be used under formal and limited licence arrangements arranged through our **Dulux** Select Decorator scheme, where the paints used must have been manufactured by our company. If you do have any interest in joining that scheme, the information is available on our website: www.duluxselectdecorators.co.uk

We do wish you every success in your growing business and in developing your new concepts for your clientele. Incidentally, if you do decide to pursue your creative idea under the name of "Howard Hues", you may want to register this name as a trademark, which would be the appropriate way to protect the name and secure your rights in it. You could arrange this yourself at limited cost by contacting the Patent Office, where the advice teams are always helpful and willing to advise small companies and innovators. Their website is: www.patent.gov.uk or their telephone number 0845 9 500 505 (UK callers only - charged at local rate).

Thank you for your interest.

Yours sincerely

D. Franklin

Dawn M. Franklin
Patent & Trade Marks Department

"Cookeswithin"
99, Kerching Drive
Twickenham, Middx, UK

Dawn M. Franklin
Patent and Trade Marks Department,
ICI paints
PO Box 1883,
Wexham Road,
Slough PDO
Berks SL2 5FD

4th July

Your Ref: M-260-SL

Dear Dawn,

Thank you for your kind reply to my letters. Might I say first that I noted your splendid name? Are you from America? What does the M stand for? It must me something of which you are quite proud since you use it so prominently in your signature. And here am I writing to you on 4th July, Independence Day. Amazing or what?

However, I think my letter to you may have confused you a little. It was addressed to Bob Hughes on the envelope and then in the letter to Mr Howard. Yes I am Bob Howard, that is correct, but *Hughes* was *Hues*, as in colour textures, and not another alternative name. How confusing would that be if I tried to write to you using a false name? The postman who delivered was a little perplexed too. "Who are you today?" he quipped, offering me your letter.

I noted with interest your comments regarding the Dulux logo on my vans, and I can assure you that I have no intention of breaking the law or going against your instructions. But what guarantee do I have now? Having explained my ideas to you regarding *"Howard Hues"*, there is nothing to stop you using these as and when you like. I could find that after some time has passed, you will bring out a range of specialized colours that too closely resemble my *"Howard Hues"* range. And with your advertising and marketing budgets, you could simply "blow me out of the water!" Who's to say that my *Credit Card Red*, and *Lib. Dem. Yellow* won't be used by you in the future? It would be good to have some reassurance on this.

I appreciate your advice on the Patenting of my name, but as you will understand I was expecting some better news from you, with a chance that we could have become successful partners.

I may well try some other paint manufacturers first, but if I could have reassurances from you that you won't steal my ideas, I would be very grateful. I hope to hear from you with the answers to my many questions.

Kind Regards,

Yours sincerely

Bob Howard
Bob Howard

ICI Group Intellectual Property

PO Box 1883
Wexham Road
Slough PDO
Berkshire SL2 5FO
England

Telephone (01753) 550000
Fax (01753) 677247

Your ref.	Our ref. M-260-SL (Please Quote)	Direct Dial 01753 877235	Date 7th July

Dear Mr Howard

Howard Hues paint colours

Please accept my apologies for inadvertently addressing you incorrectly in my last letter. Clearly the play on words in your proposed project of ""Howards Hughes" was very effective and remained in my subconscious as I typed your address. I trust that your postman will be reassured that you have retained your original identity.

As for my name and its origins, I am British but the name Franklin has a long history and has a prominence in American history too (e.g. Benjamin Franklin) and I have many connections with America, so perhaps that has increased the likelihood of your expecting me to be an American.

You ask what guarantee you have that ICI will not copy the ideas you have revealed in your original letter. Firstly, I can assure you that ICI is a reputable company that treats seriously all Intellectual Property rights and would not seek to infringe any rights you may have.

Secondly, you wisely did not reveal any detailed analysis of the shades of colours you would have in your range, so there is no possibility that we could reproduce those.

Thirdly, as soon as you secure registration of the name ""Howards Hughes" as a trade mark, your rights in that name would be legally protected and other companies, ICI included, could not adopt the same or a similar name in relation to paints.

Finally, it would be possible for you to protect the individual colour names in the same way via trade mark registration to prevent anyone else adopting the same names, although this would perhaps be beyond your initial budget. As far as ICI is concerned, I can confirm that we will not be adopting any of the names you have listed.

I trust that this provides you with the reassurance you requested and wish you success in your business endeavours.

Yours sincerely

D Franklin

Dawn M. Franklin
Patent & Trade Marks Department

"Cookeswithin"
99, Kerching Drive
Twickenham, Middx, UK.

Dawn M. Franklin
Patent and Trade Marks Department,
ICI paints
PO Box 1883,
Wexham Road,
Slough PDO
Berks SL2 5FD

13th July   Your Ref: M-260-SL

Dear Dawn,

Thank you so much for your letter dated 7th July. And thank you for answering all of my questions especially those of your American heritage. I found that particularly interesting.

Your advice on secure registration was indescribably valuable and I think I will start to investigate protecting my new brand of "Howard Hues" immediately.

Did you notice your mistake again? You wrote <u>Howards Hughes</u> twice! Hey, but who's counting?

Apart from thanking you, and churlishly mentioning again the difference between Hughes and Hues (petty I know) I wanted to let you know about another idea I've had that I feel would be incredibly popular and profitable both for me and Dulux.

I want to start a range of colours that I'm going to call " Shades of Rock". Have you noticed how many bands have colours in their names? There are so many. How brilliant would it be to go into Homebase and buy a tin of Black Sabbath, Deep Purple, Pink Floyd, or Simply Red? Or find on display at B & Q tins of Moody Blues, Barry White, James Brown and David Grey? It's incredible don't you think?

Just imagine the TV advertising. Forget that shaggy dog you use. You could have the real thing with all those amazing Rock and Pop stars endorsing their own colours and shades. Ozzie Osborne would be great advertising paint don't you think?

I have included with this letter a colour chart which will be the beginnings of "The Shades of Rock", and wondered if you would be interested in this by way of a partnership? Perhaps this is the better one to begin with, and from here depending on the success (of which I have no doubt) we could then discuss again my "Howard Hues" range.

I have included another Invoice for the range in case you are interested and I look forward to hearing from you hopefully with some positive and encouraging news on our potentially profitable partnership together. I remain forever hopeful.

Kindest Regards

Yours sincerely

Bob Howard

Bob Howard.

Sales Invoice

Date: _____ Invoice No: _____

From: "Cookeswithin" 99, Kerching Drive,
Twickenham, Middx, UK

Qty	Description	Amount exclusive of V.A.T. £	V.A.T. Net £
	Costs for Bob Howard's Shades of Rock Colour paint range.		
	Individual shades per tin		£15.00p
	Barry White range		£57.99p
	The whole range of 20 colours		£299.00p
	As with most Rock / Pop related matters, I am prepared to donate 15% to Charity once we have struck up a deal.		
		Sub total exc. V.A.T. £	
		V.A.T. £	
		Total due £	

V.A.T. rate..............................
Payment terms.......................
Tax Point...............................

Bob Howard's SHADES OF ROCK Colour Chart

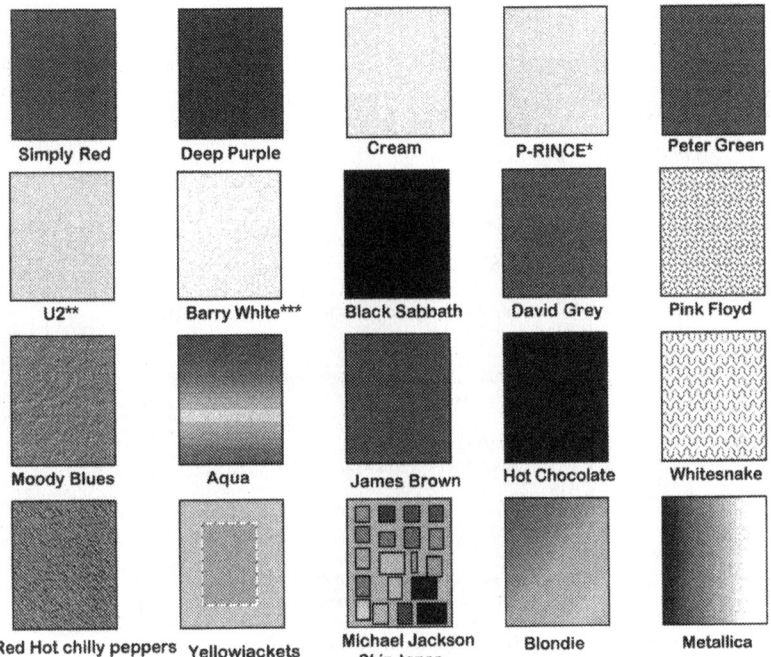

* Otherwise know as Pale Blue.

** Undercoat only

*** Only available in very large tins

Go to www.invoicebook.com for a full-colour version of this chart – Ed

ICI Group Intellectual Property

PO Box 1883
Wexham Road
Slough PDO
Berkshire SL2 5FO
England

Telephone (01753) 550000
Fax (01753) 877247

Your ref.	Our ref. M-260-SL (Please Quote)	Direct Dial 01753 877235	Date 14th July

Dear Mr Howard

Howard Hues paint colours

Thank you for your letter dated 13th July. I am pleased that you found the guidance on trade mark protection to be useful.

My first reference to "Howard Hughes" in my letter of 7th July was intentional as I was at that point in my letter referring specifically to the play on words, rather than to your project. Perhaps that would have been absolutely clear if I had been more precise in my grammar and written the sentence as:

Clearly the play on words of "Howard Hughes" in your proposed project called "Howard Hues" was very effective...etc.

My second reference was unintentional as you rightly would expect to protect "Howard Hues" as your trade mark but as you have kindly said "who's counting?"

As for your latest creative idea on colour naming, unfortunately neither we nor other paint companies would be able to pursue such an idea, even if we had an interest, because the rock bands to which you refer all have significant reputations. By adopting any of their names in this way to promote our own products, even though they are in different fields of activity, would expose the company to criticism and potential threats of legal action on the grounds that such use unfairly trades on the reputation of the rock bands. The consent of the individual bands would be required and, if obtainable, which is unlikely, would be prohibitively expensive. Regrettably, this idea is therefore unlikely to be worth your pursuing.

As for future co-operation in the creation of new colours and colour names, I have to say that it is highly unlikely that ICI would have an interest in developing a partnership. We have established teams of professionally-qualified people working on the development of our paint ranges with long-term strategies in place for the DULUX brand. You may find that smaller companies may have more opportunities to adopt your creative ideas.

I hope that this disappointing news is not too discouraging for you and that you will eventually find a suitable partner with whom you can achieve success.

Yours sincerely

Dawn M. Franklin
Patent & Trade Marks Department

"TREETOPS", 58 SPITFIRE CLOSE, SOUTH CROYDON, SURREY

Customer Services
Southern Trains
PO Box 277
Tonbridge
TN9 2ZP

Dear Southern,

When you took over from the appalling Network South Central, I along with many, many other regular rail users had high hopes for the end to our dark travel nightmare that had reduced us over a number of years to sullen, cowed sheep.

There were early signs that signalled a new era in the commuter rail experience. There was a smart new dark green livery that helped to erase traumatic memories of the old blue and yellow. There was shiny new rolling stock – albeit hermetically sealed carriages with no windows to open when the heating becomes unbearable. (I notice by the way that the automatic doors seem to jam with frightening regularity, and find myself wondering how I would escape in an emergency. Last Thursday I caught myself looking around for a fire extinguisher to hurl through the window if need be. I even speculated on the strength required to wrench the parcel shelves from their moorings to use as a battering ram ...)

Most significantly of all, these new carriages have far fewer seats than the old 'slam' door trains, and no overhead means of support when standing. It was thus with a sinking heart that I finally managed – after much pushing and shouts of "Could you move down please?" – to heave my way onto a rush hour train where eight carriages worth of commuters were crammed into the paltry four provided. Not only was the crush suffocating and the heat stifling, but the whole journey was made all the more intolerable by taking twice as long as normal (due apparently to the wrong kind of snow on the rails).

I am a patient person, but it seems to me that the time has come to fight fire with fire. On no less than nine occasions this year you apparently have seen fit to charge me a premium rate for travelling during the rush hour, but have not felt obligated to provide any more than off-peak rolling stock. I am therefore introducing my own 'Fair's fare' scheme. I am sending you an invoice for these journeys for a sum representing the difference between a full fare and an off-peak fare. I have added a small amount to cover due wear and tear on my clothing, my legs and my blood pressure. I trust you will find this acceptable and look forward to receiving the first of what will undoubtedly be many instalments.

Yours faithfully

Bob Johnstone
Bob Johnstone

P.S
'Fair's fare' is my own invention, and if you use it I will invoice you for that too.

Sales Invoice

Invoice No: BOB 002
Date:
From: "Treetops" Spitfire Close, South Croydon, Surrey

Qty	Description	Amount exclusive of V.A.T. £	V.A.T. Net £
	Refund due to provision of inadequate rolling stock between Sanderstead and Victoria		
	Peak rate return fares from Sanderstead to Victoria 9 x £10.10		£90.90
	Minus amount due for off-peak return fares from Sanderstead to Victoria 9 x £8.00		-£72.00
	Sub total:		£18.90
	Divided by 2 to calculate one-way amount		
	Cheques payable to Bob Johnstone		
		Sub total exc. V.A.T.£	
		V.A.T.£	
		Total due£	£9.45

V.A.T. rate..........................
Payment terms.....................
Tax Point ....

Southern
Customer Services
PO Box 277
Tonbridge
Kent TN9 2ZP

Ref: 595838E / C929172

Mr Bob Johnstone
'Treetops'
58 Spitfire Close
South Croydon
Surrey

8 April

Dear Mr Johnstone

Thank you for your letter of 4 April

I am sorry you are not happy with the service we provided and can understand your frustration. We would ideally like to be able to provide a seat for all our passengers. However, as you have experienced, many services have people standing on them every day. Whilst we are running more services now than ever before and have all available carriages in operation during peak times, the increase in demand over recent years has grown such that it has exceeded these improvements. We regularly monitor the number of people on each train and we do make changes to the service where we can, although we are limited to the amount of stock we currently have.

We do plan for a degree of standing during the morning and evening peak period on many services, especially in the inner suburban areas, but we monitor all our passenger loadings regularly and try to distribute our rolling stock in an effort to avoiding excessive crowding on any particular service. We are aware of sustained growth on many of our services, and I have passed your comments to our planning department so they can take them into account when deciding where extra stock is needed. Unfortunately, as every serviceable train is in operation during the rush hour, lengthening of a particular train can only be achieved by shortening another.

Trains can become more crowded than usual for a number of reasons. If there have been earlier cancellations, then trains will inevitably carry more than the usual number of passengers. Occasionally, trains will have fewer coaches than usual because units have been temporarily withdrawn from service for emergency repairs, often as a result of vandalism. Every effort is made to return these defective units back to service as quickly as possible.

We are working towards improving the situation, but I am afraid it is not something that can change overnight. As part of the £1 billion order for new trains we placed when we took over the franchise, which is for over 700 new carriages, some are included to tackle this issue.

These new trains, which have already replaced a significant number of older slam door trains across our network, are being delivered as quickly as possible. It is hoped that they will all be in service by the Summer and the additional carriages will be used where demand is highest.

I must point out that unfortunately unless you have a seat reservation we are unable to guarantee to provide you with a seat for your journey. Therefore I am unable to consider a refund on this occasion.

Please accept my apologies for the problems you have experienced whilst travelling with Southern recently. We are committed to providing a good service for everyone who travels with us.

Once again, I am sorry for the inconvenience you have been caused. I hope that your future dealings with Southern are of a higher standard.

If I can be of any further assistance, please do not hesitate to write to me at the above address.

Yours sincerely

Camille Thomas
Southern Customer Services

"TREETOPS", 58 SPITFIRE CLOSE, SOUTH CROYDON, SURREY

Camille Thomas
Southern Customer Services
PO Box 277
Tonbridge
Kent TN9 2ZP

Dear Camille

Thank you so much for your long, explanatory reply to my original letter and invoice. You asked me to write to you again for further assistance, and so this is what I am doing. It seems the nub of your difficulty is a lack of rolling stock and that "lengthening of a particular train can only be achieved by shortening another". I have every sympathy with your plight. In fact I have personal experience of the problem you face.

You see I am a model railway enthusiast of some half a century's experience (OO Gauge). Indeed I have a layout that replicates in miniature the journey from East Grinstead to London. As you can imagine, building an exact replica of Clapham Junction was no mean feat, and meant taking over our main bedroom, much to my wife Dierdre's consternation. In fact, I suspect she is responsible for some of the vandalism that I too have experienced on my railway. Anyway, the point is many's the time I've had to take Pullman carriages from my 'Brighton Belle' and once even an Ohio & Pacific caboose to provide for the 8.19 from Sanderstead to Victoria.

Indeed, it was this acquisition of rolling stock from elsewhere that gave me the answer to your problems. I have a colleague who is a volunteer on the Bluebell Railway. As you know, they restore old carriages (some dating back to the 1950s) to their former glory to run on their line. Now, the Bluebell line is actually very close to East Grinstead...

Yes, you've guessed it, Camille! I have actually negotiated the hire and regular use of one of the Bluebell carriages, which could be hooked onto the end of the train of yours I regularly catch to provide me with a seat. Of course, I'm not selfish, and would be quite prepared to allow you to sell special tickets to other passengers who would like a guaranteed seat in this way. You could even turn it into a feature. Naturally there are a few logistics to be ironed out. Being semi-retired I only travel to London twice a week, but such details can be overcome with some judicious time-tabling.

Can you see how this is the answer? I hope you are as excited by the prospect as I am! I think this is such a wonderful solution that I am prepared to cancel my previous invoice and instead am sending you a new one for the cost of the carriage hire; a sum which you will soon recoup through additional special ticket sales.

I look forward to hearing from you.

Bob Johnstone
Bob Johnstone

Sales Invoice

Invoice No: BOB 019

Date: _____

From: "Treetops" Spitfire Close, South Croydon, Surrey

Qty	Description	Amount exclusive of V.A.T. £	V.A.T. Net £
	Hire of a 1961 BR 'compartment' carriage		
	2 days per week for trial period of 3 months (12 weeks) @ £221.25 per day (excluding delivery to East Grinstead)		
	Cheques payable to Bob Johnstone		
		Sub total exc. V.A.T. £	
		V.A.T. £	
		Total due £	£5310

V.A.T. rate..........................

Payment terms....................

Tax Point ....

Southern
Customer Services
PO Box 277
Tonbridge
Kent TN9 2ZP

Ref: 595838E / C934157

Mr Bob Johnstone
'Treetops'
58 Spitfire Close
South Croydon
Surrey

08 June

Dear Mr Johnstone

Thank you for your letter of 22 May addressed to my colleague, Camille Thomas.

Your last letter was actually referred to me for review and I am afraid that my judgment was that no reply was called for. On reviewing the matter again it seems to me that this is still the case. Nevertheless, I note what you say.

Thank you for making contact with us again.

Yours sincerely

Richard Lancaster
Southern Customer Services

"TREETOPS", 58 SPITFIRE CLOSE, SOUTH CROYDON, SURREY

Richard Lancaster
Southern Customer Services
PO Box 277
Tonbridge
Kent TN9 2ZP

Dear Richard

Thank you so much for your kind and courteous reply to my last letter to your colleague, Camille Thomas.

It's a bit of a shame that Camille is no longer 'in the loop', as it were, as I thought we were getting along rather well. However, I quite understand that when you receive proposals as exciting and momentous as mine, it needs to be passed up the chain of command to be dealt with at the highest level.

This has actually worked out for the best, because I have realised – as no doubt did you – that my earlier proposal was flawed. Yes, Richard, you were right in your judgement of giving it the thumbs down. I gather that was your judgement because I suspect that you did not want to hurt my feelings by outright rejection and so chose to let me down gently by not replying. I understand. However, if we are to take things further I would encourage you to be more candid in future. I thrive on constructive criticism!

So here's my new proposal. I think you're going to like this a lot. A lot more practical than the extra private coach idea – and a lot less expensive!

In addition to model railways, my other passion in life is horticulture. Specifically growing geraniums. It came to me as I was giving them their Biofeed that this was the perfect solution to commuter frustration. Why not put plant pots and hanging baskets on your station platforms and then provide your customers with all they need to tend them?

It was help pass the time, it would engage them in a wonderfully creative therapy, and it would beautify all our lives. Good for the commuters, good for Southern, and good for the environment! Now, isn't that a winner? All I ask is that I become your preferred supplier of geraniums for the East Grinstead to Victoria line.

I look forward to hearing your reaction with eager anticipation.

Yours sincerely

Bob Johnstone

Bob Johnstone.

Southern
Customer Services
PO Box 277
Tonbridge
Kent TN9 2ZP

Ref: 595838E / C936726

Mr Bob Johnstone
'Treetops'
58 Spitfire Close
South Croydon
Surrey

30 June

Dear Mr Johnstone

Thank you for your letter of 15 June

Floral displays is a subject we can agree upon. In fact feedback from the passenger surveys we routinely carry-out echoes what you say; that we should take an opportunity to brighten-up stations in exactly that way. We're not sure about the smaller stations because a lot of them are unstaffed for significant periods each day and there is unfortunately always the ever-present risk of vandalism. However, at locations where there is a round-the-clock presence the idea is probably viable. We're therefore looking initially at East Croydon and Redhill to start-off with and then maybe we'll branch-out elsewhere.

Thanks for making contact with us again.

Yours sincerely

Richard Lancaster
Southern Customer Services

www.southernrailway.com

A wholly owned subsidiary of **GOVIA** Limited

Southern is a trading name of New Southern Railway Ltd. Registered in England under Number: 3010919
Registered Office: 3rd Floor, 41-51 Grey Street, Newcastle upon Tyne, NE1 6EE.

"Cookeswithin"
99, Kerching Drive
Twickenham, Middx, UK

Mr. Mohammed Al Fayed
Harrods Ltd
87-135 Brompton Road
Knightsbridge
London

2nd August

Omnia fieri pecuniis posunt

Dear Mr. Al Fayed,

I love Harrods! It's an amazing 5-acre department store that represents everything British! I am also very impressed with your marvellous motto: "Omnia Omnibus Ubique" – All Things, For All People, Everywhere. Mine is "Omnia fieri pecuniis posunt" – All things are financially possible. I'm sure you can agree with that? I have used my motto on many occasions and it's stood me in good stead so far.

The reason I am writing to you is to offer you something that I feel could not only benefit Harrods, but also lift your public relations to a stratospheric level and turn your motto from the heady un-reachable realms of the classics into the workable and accessible "shop-floor" of the real world. OK, so enough of the cryptic clues.

I am the proud owner/manager of Howard's Historical Thespians; A company of actors and performers striving to re-enact famous scenes from British History. Our skills are very specific, and we are known primarily for our ability to stand still and pose for long periods of time. We have recently done The Battle of Trafalgar where Nelson destroyed the French and Spanish fleets at the Battle of Trafalgar, but was killed in the process in 1805, for a well-known department store in Barcelona. Also the signing of The Magna Carter – The Great Charter of English Liberty granted (under considerable duress) by King John at Runnymede on June 15, 1215, at a trade show in Berwick-on Tweed. Powerful stuff I'm sure you will agree.

So here's the reason for the letter. You have probably in excess of 25 shop window displays with immediate visual access to Knightsbridge and the surrounding streets. I am proposing that we fill each of these window displays with an Historic scene from the British past using my talented and versatile performers. Calling it "Windows of History", we could do a two or three part re-enactment from the same era: Henry VIII and his many wives (including a beheading). The battle of Britain, The great Fire of London (I have fire-eaters as well). The Great Plague with live rats. The Battle of Hastings, King Arthur and his many Knights, the list is endless. You could even have a window each for Scottish, Irish, and Welsh history (to keep them happy I suppose?) It would be a mammoth hit for you as it would be for us. I have attached an invoice that details our costs and I would be delighted to hear your response to this idea and to see when we could start for you. Our "historic scenes" can last up to 6 hours without a break, as we use personally developed semi-hypnotic trance tablets that I administer to my performers before each sitting (or standing). It's painless and wears off within an hour.

Of course, should you require horses, dogs, or other animals, then we use guide ropes, and invisible suspension cables to keep their positions secure. But rest assured, it's quite safe and no one to date has been injured or hospitalised.

I trust that you will see the potentially commercial advantages of this idea and I look forward to hearing from you with some positive news.

Kind Regards

Yours sincerely

Bob Howard

Bob Howard

Omnia fieri pecuniis possunt

Sales Invoice

Date: _____ Invoice No: _____

From: "Cookeswithin" 99, Kerching Drive,
      Twickenham, Middx, UK

Qty	Description	Amount exclusive of V.A.T. £	V.A.T. Net £
	Windows of History. Scenes of Great British events. To include: Actors, scene dressers, costume and make up, props, and any additional transport. Per window=	£345.99p	
	Additional animals to include horses, dogs, doves and assorted birds, monkeys, cats, rats, snakes, and insects.	£199.00p	
	Further animals can be requested and priced per metre.		
	Refreshments and rest area (within 2 minutes of Harrods) Portaloos, and tea and coffee facilities. Total per day	£56.00p	
		Sub total exc. V.A.T.£	
		V.A.T.£	
		Total due£	£600.99p

V.A.T. rate: _____
Payment terms: _____
Tax Point: _____

9th August

Dear Mr Howard,

Your letter to Mr Fayed has been passed for my attention

The Harrods windows are all supplier funded. If you were to perform a re-enactment of famous scenes from British History, this would have to be sponsored. The concept is a great one, and has in fact been undertaken in a somewhat different format on a number of occasions. For the Fantasy Garden Promotion last year, brands were able to produce a series of gardens across the Brompton Road windows, and the Diarmuid Gavin window had a number of live ducks and lambs. The LG Live windows was a huge success, whereby a family interacted, as they would in their own homes utilising the LG varied range of products, plasma screen, fridge, TV etc and included celebrities, Kim Wilde planted/tended a garden.

The Marketing plan is usually planned a year in ahead, therefore there are no opportunities are available for the remainder of the year. However, we will keep your details on file for future reference, and thank you for taking the time to write to Harrods.

Yours sincerely,
FOR HARRODS LIMITED

pp R. Harris

Mark Briggs
Visual Merchandising Director
Harrods (Management) Limited

Customer Relations,
Ikea Svenska AB,
S-343 00 Almhult,
Sweden.

"Cookeswithin"
99, Kerching Drive
Twickenham, Middx, UK

24th March

Raring Min herre eller Frun.

Hälsningarna från Förenade kungariket Storbritannien och Nordirland. JAG lita på du er har en böter dag, och så pass den hår brev vill inte förstöra den.

Now in English ...

Dear Sir or Madam.

Greetings from The United Kingdom. I trust you are having a fine day, and that this letter doesn't spoil it. That is, of course, what I tried to write to you in Swedish. I hope it was correct. and it didn't come out resembling a family insult like "Your Grandmother smells like rotten herringsæ.

It is the first time I've tried to write in Swedish, and indeed, the first time I've written to IKEA. You encourage this on your assembly instructions by saying: *"If you have any ideas which can help us to improve our assembly instructions or our products please send them to you at the above address."* So this is what I am doing.

In order for you to maintain low cost, IKEA shoppers like me are *"Pro-sumers"* – half producers, and half consumers. In other words, they have to assemble the products themselves.

So having drooled over your catalogue, I bought several items and took them home. I opened the flat packs to be greeted by a large sign saying *"FOLLOW ME"*. There was something almost spiritual about this and it made me feel quite secure and cared for. Sadly the feeling left me as quickly as it had arrived. It was a fast descent into Assembly Hell!

I started to shake uncontrollably as I checked the screws, keys, nuts, rods, and bolts, certain that there would be some missing. Bits of veneered wood that looked so inviting in the catalogue lay flat and ineffective, offering no direct inspiration as to where they went and what they did.

Some of the pictures had two men in them, whilst others had no one at all. There were electric drills hanging in mid air with no one holding them, and large crosses which I assumed were Swedish for *"DO NOT GO THERE!!"*

I tried, I really did, to get something resembling the furniture I had bought, and after three full days, I had managed a three drawer unit.

I further six days later, I had just about assembled everything I had bought, only to find that my local furniture store has almost the identical pieces, already assembled, for roughly 10% less than I had paid originally at IKEA.

So apart from boring you further with my long story of how much grief I had, I needed to explain fully the circumstances as to why I am sending you an Invoice for the difference between what I paid at IKEA, and the price my local furniture store was charging.

So the attached Invoice is the difference between your unassembled furniture and my local shop, plus assorted extras (including six left over screws). I trust that you will see that this makes sense, and I look forward to hearing from you in due course.

I will happily send you a photograph of my assembled units if that would help?

Yours most sincerely (Din mest uppriktigt)

Bob Howard

Sales Invoice

Date: _____ Invoice No: _____

From: "Cookeswithin" 99, Kerching Drive,
Twickenham, Middx, UK

Qty	Description	Amount exclusive of V.A.T. £	V.A.T. Net £
	Final costs from Ikea of assorted furniture as detailed in above letter.	£4,768.99p	
	Local furniture store: Cost of identical (almost) items Fully assembled, delivered, and unboxed. £4,300.76p		
	Difference between Ikea and local store	£468.23p	
	Cost of pick up (petrol only), additional roof rack, And careful Disposal of cardboard boxes (A long and painful Journey to the local council tip!)	£43.99p	
	My time for two days for assembly of your products. Charged out at £16.87 pence per hour for 16 hours	£269.92p	
	Sundry extras, Band-Aids, money to swear-box, Extraction of Screwdriver from wall etc.	£41.90p	
	Sub total exc. V.A.T. £		
	V.A.T. £		
	Total due £		£824.04p

V.A.T. rate: _____
Payment terms: _____
Tax Point: _____

"Cookeswithin"
99, Kerching Drive
Twickenham, Middx, UK

Susan Tallents - HR Manager
Dearne Valley Customer Contact Centre
Unit 4 Callflex Business Park
Doncaster Road
Wath-upon-Dearne
Rotherham
S63 7DN

27th May

Dear Ms Tallents,

What a journey this has been!! And still it continues. It would have been easier to search for The Holy Grail.

As you will see from the enclosed correspondences, I have been attempting to get a response from several letters written to IKEA for the past three months.

The original letter, dated 24th March, was sent to the address I found in Sweden, and partly written in Swedish thinking that this might soften the blow, so to speak!

But no! Absolute silence.

So after much trawling, searching, E mails and general enquiries, I found your name and address claiming some qualification on Customer Services. I genuinely hope so especially after such a long time trying to find a real person from whom I could get a reply.

I look forward to hearing from you in due course. After such a long time, I hope you don't send back a simple two line "company policy" apology with no real option for a solution to my many issues with IKEA.

Yours in great anticipation.

Bob Howard

Date:

1st June

Mr B Howard
Cookeswithin
99 Kerching Drive
Twickenham
Middx

Dear Mr Howard,

Thank you for your copy letters dated 24th March, 19th April, 18th May and the most recent which is the reason I am responding addressed to Susan Tallents, HR Manager, dated 27th May

Firstly, please accept my apology on behalf of IKEA for the delay in responding to the letters which you sent direct to Sweden, these letters would have been immediately re-directed to myself in the UK, but unfortunately IKEA UK have not had sight of these previously so obviously were unable to reply to them.

I have read your correspondence and I thank you for taking the time to detail your comments in such a jocular light-hearted manner.

I will ensure that the comments in reference to the instructions of IKEA products are directed to the correct department within IKEA UK and GLOBAL IKEA.

In response to your invoice and a request for a payment from IKEA for the reason that you quote:

'Unfortunately IKEA makes no comments in relation to price or to products similar to IKEA'.

'There is no policy in force within IKEA UK to make payments to IKEA customers in relation to the duration of time IKEA products take to assemble'.

Whilst I found your letter to be 'tongue in cheek' and I do thank you for the way you have dealt with this issue, I do feel that IKEA UK are required to answer your letter quoting the policy and procedures in force within IKEA UK.

IKEA Ltd.,
Unit 4, Callflex Business Park,
Doncaster Road, Wath-upon-Dearne,
Rotherham, South Yorkshire S63 7DN
Tel: 01709 763300
Fax: 01709 763310

Registered Office:
21 Holborn Viaduct
London EC1A 2DY
Registered in England
No. 1986283

Thank you again for taking the time to detail your complaint, and I would hope that you would please accept 2 coffee and cake vouchers which can be used when you next visit an IKEA store.

Yours sincerely,

IKEA Customer Care

Enclosed 2 coffee/cake vouchers

"Cookeswithin"
99, Kerching Drive
Twickenham, Middx, UK

IKEA Ltd
Customer Contact Centre
Unit 4 Callflex Business Park
Doncaster Road
Wath-upon-Dearne
Rotherham
S63 7DN

7 June

Dear   ???   ....(indecipherable squiggle!)

Thank you for your reply dated 1st June to my many letters to IKEA. I had, as you pointed out, written to Susan Tallents, but sadly your signature doesn't give me any clues as to whom you really are. So I am unable to address you, as I would like. Dear Mister or Ms. Squiggle sounds silly, and even my gifts as an amateur handwriting buff, don't offer any clues to your gender or character.

Of course I accept your apology, but it would be nice to know where the original "Swedish" letters went. I took quite a long time translating them, and the books I used seem now somewhat redundant. Any clues who could benefit from "Teach yourself Swedish in 24 hours"? Would you like them?

I was also intrigued at the style of your letter, as it appeared that you were **SHOUTING AT ME!!!** The **BOLD** text was a little intimidating and somewhat off-putting. I would have read it just as well had it been in regular text. **Honestly!**

But more to the point was the exciting find of the two Coffee and Cake vouchers you so kindly sent. Although this doesn't in any way compensate for the trouble and costs I originally incurred, they are very welcome indeed.

I am planning a trip to USA in the next couple of weeks, and wondered if I could use them out there if I decide to visit IKEA? Would they be valid currency? The coffee and cake in America are so much nicer than here, don't you think? I can take them with me on my future trip. Another two would be great as well, as I'm taking my family and it would be great to be able to treat all four of us instead of paying for two and getting two for free.

I look forward to hearing back from you with my many questions, especially those relating to your identity and the extra cake vouchers.

Kind Regards

Yours sincerely

Bob Howard

Bob Howard

Date:

13th June

Mr B Howard
Cookeswithin
99 Kerching Drive
Twickenham
Middx

Thank you for your letter dated 7th June

Firstly, please accept our apology for the initials on the letter dated 1st June, the IKEA Customer Care Team only initial their customer care letters

If the issues they are dealing with are deemed to be of a serious nature, then the IKEA Customer Care Team sign in full, for and on behalf of Peter Hogsted, Retail Manager, IKEA UK.

I do hope that this clarifies the situation.

Unfortunately, IKEA UK has no knowledge as to the whereabouts of the letters you sent to Sweden, so we are unable to comment further.

I have to advise you that the Coffee and Cake Vouchers are not accepted outside of the UK, but I have taken the liberty of enclosing another two, in the hope you and your family will visit an IKEA store in the UK in the near future.

I do not feel it prudent to continue with further correspondence in relation to the issues you have raised, I feel that IKEA UK has answered these in adequate detail.

Assuring you of our best attention at all times,

Yours si
IKEA C

IKEA Ltd.,
Unit 4, Callflex
Doncaster Road,
Rotherham, Sou
Tel: 01709 7633
Fax: 01709 7633

"Cookeswithin"
99, Kerching Drive
Twickenham, Middx, UK

Peter Hogsted
Customer Contact Centre
Unit 4 Callflex Business Park
Doncaster Road
Wath-upon-Dearne
Rotherham
S63 7DN

22nd June

Dear Mr. Hogsted

Thank you very much for the 4 Coffee and Cake vouchers which I now have. I am very grateful. Although this cannot possibly be seen as even the smallest degree of compensation for the time I have spent assembling your furniture, it is a gesture nonetheless which I accept.

Assuming of course that these are genuine vouchers and not simply pieces of yellow card run on for my benefit on your photocopying machine, is there any way I could get a small note from you to verify them in case I was asked at the counter? That would be very helpful and prevent any further embarrassment between IKEA and me.

I hope you will find the enclosed instructions informative and useful.

They should be included with each voucher to show customers that IKEA do in fact have a sense of humour and can laugh at, and with, their complex system of assembly which has caused me such grief and angst. I have enclosed an Invoice for this idea assuming that you will in fact want to use them.

Finally, it would be good to hear back from you just to make sure there are no hard feelings.

Kind Regards,

Yours sincerely,

Bob Howard

Sales Invoice

Date:
From:
Invoice No:

Qty	Description	Amount exclusive of V.A.T.£	V.A.T. Net £
	Design and lay out costs for Instructions on "How to use the IKEA Coffee and Cake Vouchers"	£60.00p	
	Time and materials	£90.00p	
	Additional Software		
	Swedish translation charges (Ms. Olga Schmoergenberg)	£35.00p	
	Total payable	£185.00p	

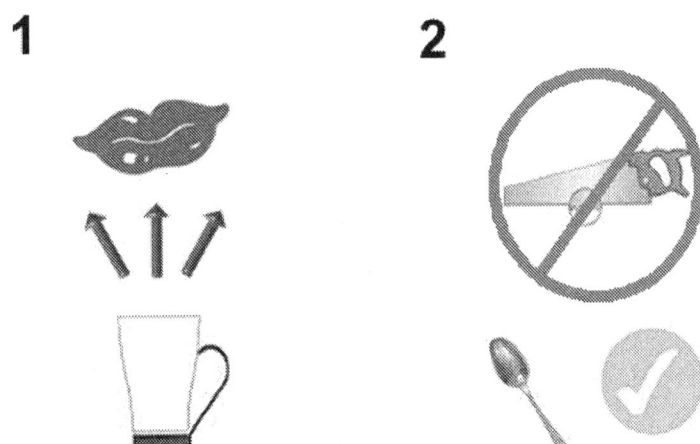

Coffee and Cake instructions

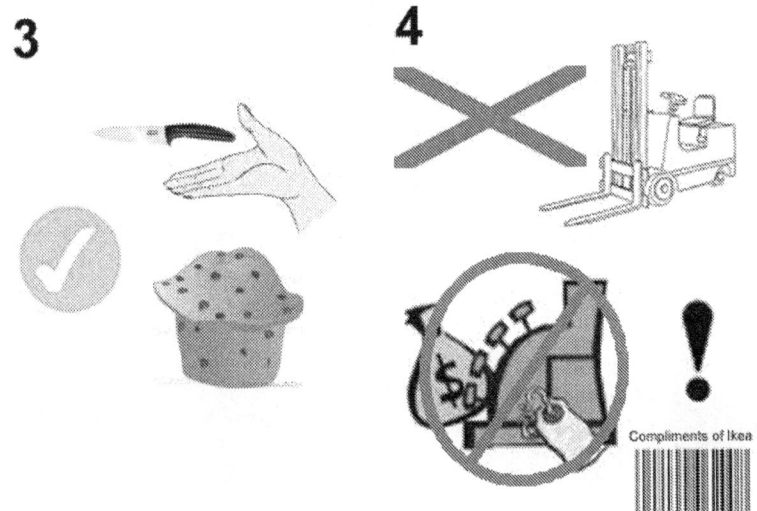

Compliments of Ikea

Date:

24th June

Mr B Howard
Cookeswithin
99 Kerching Drive
Twickenham
Middx

Dear Mr Howard,

Thank you for your letter dated 22nd June

Please accept this letter as confirmation that the 4 Coffee and Cake Vouchers issued to you from IKEA Customer Care Team are valid and can be used in any IKEA store.

Thank you for taking the time to detail your complaint and your comments have been noted.

Regards

IKEA Customer Care

IKEA Ltd.,
Unit 4, Callflex Business Park,
Doncaster Road, Wath-upon-Dearne,
Rotherham, South Yorkshire S63 7DN
Tel: 01709 763300
Fax: 01709 763310

Registered Office:
21 Holborn Viaduct
London EC1A 2DY
Registered in England
No. 1986283

Inter IKEA Systems B.V.

Mr B Howard
Cookeswithin
99 Kerching Drive
Twickenham
Middx

Delft, July 19

Dear Mr. Howard,

This is in response to your last communication in letter of May 27. We do apologize for the delay in responding to you, but unfortunately your letter has circulated between different IKEA offices until finally reaching this desk. We are sorry for any inconvenience.

We would like to confirm receipt of your above letter and would like to thank you for taking your time to write to us about your experience with shopping at IKEA U.K.

As the world-wide franchisor of The IKEA Concept we are happy that IKEA customers bring their concerns to our attention. It is customer feedback like yours that enables us to take action to do a better job in the future.

We have passed on your letter to the Retail Manager of IKEA Ltd., who is the owner and operator of the IKEA Franchise in United Kingdom, for information and action.

We hope that the matter will be solved in a satisfactory manner. If this should not be the case, please do not hesitate to contact us again and thank you once more for writing to us.

Sincerely Yours,
Inter IKEA Systems B.V.

on behalf of Mikael Bartroff
Director Franchising Division

Merete Jakobsen (Ms.)
Assistant

cc.: Retail Manager, IKEA Ltd., United Kingdom.

Postal address
Inter IKEA Systems B.V.
Olof Palmestraat 1
NL - 2616 LN Delft
The Netherlands

Telephone
+31 15 2153815

Telefax
+31 15 2153838

Bank
Account no. 25.31.66.985
Fortis Bank (Nederland) N.V.
Rotterdam, The Netherlands

IBAN
NL04FTSB0253166985
BIC / SWIFT
FTSBNL2R

Org No.
27232886
EU VAT No.
NL006784926B01

"Cookeswithin"
99, Kerching Drive
Twickenham, Middx, UK

Mikael Bartroff
Director Franchising Division,
Inter IKEA Systems B.V.
Olof Palmestraat 1,
NL-2616 LN Delft,
The Netherlands.

1st August .

Dear Mikael,

"Dank u definitief voor uw antwoord aan mijn brief van 27 Mei . Ik was geschokt en verrast om het te ontvangen maar wilde eerst u in het Nederlands als gebaar van goodwill en aan de gang zijnde vriendschap tussen onze landen danken." Thank you finally for your reply to my letter of 27th May. I was shocked and surprised to receive it but wanted first to thank you in Dutch as a gesture of goodwill and on-going friendship between our countries. (Impressed?)

I have had several correspondences with IKEA Ltd here in UK and their customer services have been courteous and reasonably understanding throughout.

Whereas to date I have received 4 coffee and cake vouchers from IKEA, the furniture I originally purchased is lying in a disorganised heap in my cellar. I can't and will never be able to assemble it. I have sought counselling and help from my local church. I have tried anger management classes. I have even attended a couple of furniture woodwork seminars at the technical college, but sadly all to no avail. My dreams of a better future with IKEA have been shattered.

Do you want it back? I can sell it to you at a much-reduced price. Apart from a couple of grub screws and a bent hinge bracket, it's all intact and as supplied. I have included another invoice in case we can come to some arrangement.

I would be more than happy to drive it across to you so you can see how difficult this has been for me. It would give me a valuable and well-deserved break. Could you send me some directions from the UK to your offices, please? Let me know when you are free to spend say a morning taking back my IKEA goods and we can hopefully put this whole sorry affair behind us. I look forward to your reply hopefully sometime within the next six months.

Kind regards and please thank Merete for her drafting of your letter and pert signature on your behalf. I would be more than happy to say: "Goede dag, en hoe over koffie en cake op deze fijne Dinsdag ochtend die gebruikt natuurlijk mijn aquired onlangs bons IKEA?" Good day, and how about coffee and cake on this fine Tuesday morning, using of course my newly acquired IKEA vouchers?

Sincerely Yours,

Bob Howard

Sales Invoice			
Date:		Invoice No:	
From:			
Qty	Description	Amount exclusive of V.A.T. £	V.A.T. Rate £
	Return of IKEA Goods of what promised to be: A Three drawer Unit, several chairs, a table, another cupboard, And a medium sized wardrobe.	£89.37p	
	Boxes and accessories, screws, and Instructions (Hah!)	£21.99p	
	Petrol expenses to Delft, Holland	£78.60p	

"TREETOPS", 58 SPITFIRE CLOSE, SOUTH CROYDON, SURREY

Ken Livingstone
Lord Mayor of London
City Hall
The Queen's Walk
London SE1 2AA

Dear Mr Livingstone

I am writing to you regarding a subject that will be close to your heart (and wallet), namely the huge cost of upkeep for all street furniture within our capital. I am not talking about utilitarian items such as benches, hanging baskets and the like. I am thinking of the vast number of statues that populate all areas of central London, from historic effigies such as Sir Winston Churchill in Parliament Square to Peter Pan in Kensington Gardens.

It occurs to me that enormous sums must be spent annually, not just in cleansing and maintenance (being stationary, they are particularly vulnerable to soiling from the scourge of those filthy parasitic pigeons that infest our town), but also in commissioning new works. I have no idea how much 'Ecce Homo' in Trafalgar Square cost, but given that the sculptor provided a mere midget I'm sure you will agree we did not get value for money. These days a Gormley, a Caro or even a Mark Reddy (are you familiar with his work?) will cost tens of thousands; money that I am sure you would rather spend on the Underground or more buses.

I have a simple solution.

For a fraction of the cost, I am prepared to come up to London on a daily basis (not weekends) and act as a living statue in any particular square in the city that you designate. Think about it! Not only can you strategically place a 'statue' wherever you need one (how handy to impress visiting dignitaries!), but that statue could change its attire and appearance on a regular basis (costume hire extra).

Let me reassure you that I am very well qualified as a statue, having spent three years at an international circus clown school and then 18 months as a statue-in-training in the piazza at Covent Garden. More recently I gained a bursary to perform as a statue in both Florence and New York. I am very excited at the prospect of this venture as no doubt you are too; one that will not only enliven many of London's more humdrum areas, but also deliver huge savings to you during your tenure as Lord Mayor. I enclose a pro-forma invoice for a 3-month trial period in eager anticipation of your commission.

I remain your obedient servant

Bob Johnstone

Bob Johnstone

Sales Invoice

Invoice No: BOB 018

Date: _____

From: "Treetops" Spitfire Close, South Croydon, Surrey

Qty	Description	Amount exclusive of V.A.T. £	V.A.T. Net £
	Appearing as a living statue on a daily basis (Mon – Fri only) for a period not exceeding 3 months, in and around central London (suburbs negotiable)		
	June – August 2005: 65 days @ £75 per day	£4875.00	
	Travel expenses ('Off Peak) 65 days @ £6 per day travelcard	£390.00	
	Normal attire will be provided F.O.C. Any special requirements (Military uniform, period dress etc) will be quoted separately per item specified		
	Personal insurance, covering interference, molestation and/or physical assault, but not including verbal taunts or abuse.	£45.00	
	Cheques payable to Bob Johnstone		
		Sub total exc. V.A.T £	
		V.A.T £	
		Total due £	£5310

V.A.T. rate...........................
Payment terms.......................
Tax Point ....

GREATER **LONDON** AUTHORITY

Mayor's Office

City Hall
The Queen's Walk
London SE1 2AA
Switchboard: 020 7983 4000
Minicom: 020 7983 4458
Web: www.london.gov.uk

Bob Johnstone
'Treetops'
58 Spitfire Close
South Croydon
Surrey

Our ref:
Your ref:
Date: 3 May
Re-sent: 3 June

Dear Mr. Johnstone

Thank you very much for your recent letter to the Mayor concerning the cost of maintaining statues and your kind offer to work as a living statue.
Please accept my reply on Mr. Livingstone's behalf.

Your idea is interesting and we will keep your details on file should the occasion arise where your services would be appropriate.

Thank you for writing and showing your interest and taking the time to write to the Mayor.

Yours sincerely

Sarah Atkinson
Cultural Strategy Administration Officer

Direct telephone: 020 7983 4777 Fax: 020 7983 4706, Email: **Sarah.Atkinson**@london.gov.uk

"TREETOPS", 58 SPITFIRE CLOSE, SOUTH CROYDON, SURREY

Sarah Atkinson
Cultural Strategy Administration Officer
Mayor's Office, Greater London Authority
City Hall, The Queen's Walk
London SE1 2AA

Dear Sarah

Thank you so much for your encouraging letter. I had almost given up hope of a reply, but then your kind and thoughtful note popped through my letterbox! How silly of me to imagine that Mr Livingstone would have time to respond in person. How busy he must be with new schemes for taxing Londoners. I should have stopped to think how a man of his huge responsibilities must have a big team to whom he can delegate many matters.

I am absolutely thrilled that you are interested in my London's Living Statues™ idea, and fully understand that you want to keep the launch back for the right occasion. However, in my experience, Sarah, wonderful ideas can get forgotten in a bottom drawer unless definite plans are made whilst everyone is still filled with enthusiasm. Sadly occasions don't just arise - they have to be scheduled and put in everyone's diaries. In the case of Mr Livingstone, probably some weeks in advance.

So I've been doing some research on your behalf and have come up with a selection of suitable occasions that I think would be ideal for the London's Living Statues™ launch - or 'unveiling' as I prefer to call it. Here are some to choose from:

26th July: George Bernard Shaw born in 1856
7th August: Act of Parliament in 1840 to stop the use of boys as chimney sweeps
29th Sept: Horatio Nelson born in 1758
5th Oct: The world's first bathing costume on sale in London in 1830

I am sure you can see how each of these events would provide wonderfully inspiring subjects for an unveiling, although modelling a costume by the Serpentine in October might prove rather chilly! Anyway if you could let me know which you prefer, I will set to work on the appropriate costume straight away.

By the way, I am greatly taken with your logo, and have decided to adopt one of my own. I hope this doesn't break any trademarks of yours!

Yours sincerely

Bob Johnstone
BOB **JOHNST**ONE

"Cookeswithin"
99, Kerching Drive
Twickenham, Middx, UK

Dan Brown,
Doubleday Publishing,
Random House Inc.,
1745 Broadway,
New York.
New York 10019
USA.

12th May

Dear Mr. Brown,

Firstly may I congratulate you on the great success with your books. I heard many people talking about your publications and in particular *The Da Vinci Code*. So much so, I decided to purchase a copy and read it whilst travelling to America by boat.

All appeared well at first and I started to read eagerly, hungrily, avidly, possibly ferociously. This was a serious page turner and I read on not wanting to put the book down, but at the same time, not wanting to finish it too quickly either. I reached page 226. Robert and Sophie had just reached Chateau Villette to meet Sir Leigh Teabing (odd name?): *"Sophie was comfortable in the drawing room staring into the growing fire. Beneath the Egyptian goddess, inside the fireplace, two stone gargoyles served as andirons, their mouths gaping to reveal their menacing breath, and glanced up the long nave toward the main altar in the distance."*

I'd lost something in an instant. It was only when I looked up at the page numbers did I realize that page 226 went straight to page 399!!! Help! What was I to do? I couldn't get another copy; I was at sea in more ways that one!! I had missed out on over 100 pages of the story. It was a sad state of affairs. I had to put the book down, as there seemed no real point in continuing.

So the reason for writing to you is two fold. Firstly to ask you what was in the missing pages so I can continue the book at some time, if I can be bothered of course, and secondly, to ask you to cover the time I spent reading up to page 226. It's obviously not your fault but I don't know who else I to whom I can write to relate my tale of woe. I am a slow reader, so in total it took around 5 days to read up to the point where I could go no further. I ended up reading a Barbara Cartland novel, *Lord Ravenscar's Revenge*, for the rest of the journey that wasn't that good, but it at least had all of its pages.

I know that you will sympathize with my problem, and hopefully settle my outstanding costs as detailed in the attached invoice.

Thank you and keep up the good work. Next time, I will check that all of the pages are there and in the right order.

Kindest Regards
Yours sincerely,

Bob Howard

Sales Invoice

Date:
From:
Invoice No:

Qty	Description	Amount exclusive of V.A.T. £	V.A.T. Net £
	5 days of reading up to page 226 of The Da Vinci Code, only to discover that there were 171 missing pages. Per day	£110.00p	
		£600.00p	
	Total costs		
	Barbara Cartland novel "Lord Ravenscar's revenge"	£6.99p	
		£606.99p	
	Total payable		

July 11

Bob Howard
"Cookeswithin"
99 Kerching Drive
Twickenham, Middx

Dear Mr. Howard,

Thank you very much for taking the time to write to author Dan Brown, and we apologize for the delay in sending a response.

As you can imagine, Doubleday has received an enormous volume of correspondence addressed, in our care, to Mr. Brown. While the mail has been overwhelming at times, in the past he has always devoted substantial time to reading and answering letters.

During the past year, however, Doubleday has decided <u>not</u> to forward any new correspondence to Mr. Brown, as he has been in isolation writing and focusing completely on his new novel. We hope you will understand the reason why your mail was unable to be forwarded, and we sincerely regret any further inconvenience our delay in responding might have caused you. Enclosed is another copy of THE DA VINCI CODE in the hopes that it will serve as ample compensation for your troubles.

Again, thank you for your incredible support of Dan Brown's books – we hope to have a thrilling new novel available in the near future!

Sincerely,

Jenny Choi
Doubleday Editorial

"Cookeswithin"
99, Kerching Drive
Twickenham, Middx, UK.

Ms. Jean Whitnall,
UK Sales & Marketing Director
Religious Division
Hodder & Stoughton Publishers,
338 Euston Road,
London
NW1 3BH,

25th May

Dear Ms. Whitnall,

Congratulations on the amazing success of the New International Version of The Bible. I knew that I had to write to you when I found out that you were involved as Sales and Marketing Director at Hodder & Stoughton. I hope that you can find the time to read this letter and appreciate the huge potential of this new idea I have had.

As you know, there are many translations of the Bible but one area that has been neglected to date is the translation of the Bible for the corporate user. Considering that in England alone, we have millions of corporate employees in Government, Law, The Health Service, Education, and Business, there is nothing that appears to meet the needs of these people. So I have started to translate what will hopefully become *"The New Corporate Bible"*.

I have a colleague that is also helping me do the translation and we intend to complete sometime this year. However, nothing is for free: *"The labourer is worthy of his hire"*, or in the New Corporate Bible translation: *"The employee, whether part-time or fully employed by an employer, has rights under the Employment Act 1952 Section 3, Sub-section 32b to receive duly negotiated and contractual remuneration after deductions of Income Tax and NIC in accordance with the obligations entered into and mutually agreed between the aforementioned parties."* I have therefore enclosed an invoice for our time to carry out this extensive but necessary task.

I have taken the trouble to translate for you **The Lord's Prayer** from Matthew Chapter 6 as an excellent example of 'corporate' which is attached.

Kind Regards

Yours sincerely

Bob Howard

Sales Invoice

Date: _____ Invoice No: _____

From: "Cookeswithin" 99, Kerching Drive,
Twickenham, Middx, UK

Qty	Description	Amount exclusive of V.A.T. £	V.A.T. Net £
	Translation of The Bible into "Corporate." List of books and order of translation:		
			£150.00p
	Genesis Matthew Exodus Mark		£134.00p
	Leviticus Luke Numbers John		£235.00p
	Deuteronomy Acts of the Apostles		£534.00p
	Joshua Romans Judges		£20.00
	I Corinthians Ruth II Corinthians		£235.00p
	I Samuel Galatians II Samuel		£278.89p
	Ephesians I Kings Philippians		£537.99p
	II Kings Colossians		£148.00p
	I Chronicles I Thessalonians		£149.00p
	II Chronicles II Thessalonians		£138.00p
	Ezra I Timothy Nehemiah		£867.00p
	II Timothy Esther Titus Job		45.00p
	Philemon Psalms Hebrews		£756.00p
	Proverbs James Ecclesiastes		£645.00p
	I Peter Song of Solomon II Peter		£199.00p
	Isaiah I John Jeremiah		£546.00p
	II John Lamentations		£332.00p
	III John Ezekiel		£109.90p
	Jude Daniel Revelation		£521.33p
	Hosea Joel Amos Obadiah		£908.67p
	Jonah Micah Nahum		£767.31p
	Habakkuk Zephaniah Haggai		57.97p
	Zechariah Malachi		£8,615.06p
	Total		£3,054.00p
	Plus materials, paper, ink, printer, pens pencils And sundry stationary		
	Sub total exc. V.A.T.£		
	V.A.T.£		
	Total due£		£11,669.06p

V.A.T. rate _____
Payment terms _____
Tax Point _____

The Lord's Prayer-Matthew Chapter 6, from The Corporate Bible.

"Our paternal male guardian whose occupancy of celestial realms is assumed to be the case on the balance of the evidence currently available at the time of making this statement, we regard with great respect and reverence the word, term or phrase by which you are known which distinguishes you from any other eternal being.

We invite the market positioning which you occupy and the area of activity within that market in which you dominate to be available both at this time and for the foreseeable future, as we give you full permission without restriction or restraint to operate as you wish, globally across all territories, maritime markets and airspaces in the same way that you operate as market leader in the heavenly areas of operation that are not under terrestrial jurisdiction.

We would kindly request within the current 24 hour trading period the sustenance in the food department that is necessary on a daily basis including statutory holidays, and we humbly request your overlooking our mistakes, misunderstandings, wrongdoings and further inappropriate behaviour during the same regular time scale.

In return and as a gesture of goodwill without prejudice, we give assurance that we shall endeavour to forego any justifiable claims and cancel any irregular debt as it occurs between any customers, clients, colleagues or associates and ourselves, thus regularising our relationship with them.

We further request that you remove any craving or desire for unhelpful attractions that may lure us in an inappropriate direction, and as far as any dark powers, forces or malign spiritual authorities are concerned, we require full and total deliverance at your earliest convenience.

We remain your humble servants and acknowledge everything as per the original brief from this time forth until further notice.

Affirming the above verbally in a corporate manner will confirm total, binding and absolute agreement."

Hodder & Stoughton *Publishers*

TELEPHONE: 020 7873 6000
FAX: 020 7873 6024

3rd November

Bob Howard
"Cookeswithin"
99 Kerching Drive
Twickenham, Middx

Dear Mr Howard

Thank you very much for contacting us in regard to *The New Corporate Bible*. We are extremely excited that you have contacted us as we have been thinking of producing a bible aimed directly at this particular market for a long time now and have been searching for the right person to handle the translation. It may be that you are just such a person.

Unfortunately we feel you may have approached the project from precisely the wrong end. In modern business the main themes are minimisation, speed, ease of use and accessibility. We would therefore suggest you aim your efforts toward the Memo Bible. We envisage you similarly minimising your invoice and look forward to seeing your resubmission.

With best luck on the job,

Abigail Ratcliffe
Assistant Editor
Hodder & Stoughton
338 Euston Road
London
NW1 3BH

Phone: 020 7873 6045
Fax: 020 7873 6059
E-mail: abigail.ratcliffe@hodder.co.uk

HODDER & STOUGHTON LTD.
REGISTERED OFFICE:
338 EUSTON ROAD
LONDON NW1 3BH
COMPANY NO: 651692 ENGLAND
www.hodder.co.uk

A MEMBER OF THE HODDER HEADLINE GROUP

"Cookeswithin"
99, Kerching Drive
Twickenham, Middx, UK

Ms. Abigail Ratcliffe
Assistant Editor
Hodder & Stoughton Publishers,
338 Euston Road,
London
NW1 3BH

11th November

Dear Abigail,

Thank you so much for your letter dated 3rd November and your creative and helpful comments.

Whereas I don't feel too discouraged that you feel I have approached the project of *The Corporate Bible* from "The wrong end", I am aware that your suggestion of *The Memo Bible* is a good one and worthy of serious consideration.

Therefore I enclose a full and unedited version of *The Memo Bible* for your consideration.

As you can imagine, I have spent some considerable time and effort on this and attempted to include all the key points from the original 66 Books. You will also notice that it fits very neatly and precisely onto a memo "post-it' pad, minimizing paper, and offering excellent value for money.

I suggest having this printed on similar memo pads with a retail-selling price of around 63 pence plus VAT.

With that in mind, I have amended and "minimized" my Invoice accordingly.

I hope that this will be of interest to you, and Hodder Publishers, and I look forward to offering *The Memo Bible* to you exclusively for future publication.

Please keep you mind open to *The Corporate Bible* as well. It has its place in today's market, as I'm sure you can appreciate.

Eagerly yours,

Bob Howard

Bob Howard

Sales Invoice

Date: _____ **Invoice No:** _____

From: "Cookeswithin" 99, Kerching Drive,
Twickenham, Middx, UK

Qty	Description	Amount exclusive of V.A.T. £	V.A.T. Net £
	To: The Memo Bible. Creative fees, construction, production and Lay out to include all materials, research, and copy.		£231.78p
	Additional materials and specific template for memo-pads		£65.99p
	Copy, spell checking, and proof reading of The Memo Bible, And final amendments where relevant and necessary.		£110.76p
	All of the above are Net costs.		
	I'm sure we can agree to offset some of these costs when we Discuss advances?		
		Sub total exc. V.A.T. £	
		V.A.T. £	
		Total due £	

V.A.T. rate: _____
Payment terms: _____
Tax Point: _____

The Memo Bible © Howard & Johnstone

I started the whole business
You screwed it up
I tried talking to you
You wouldn't listen
I sent you several memos
No reply
I sent the junior partner to sort it out
We await your response
See you later
The Boss

"TREETOPS", 58 SPITFIRE CLOSE, SOUTH CROYDON, SURREY

The Marketing Director
Automobiles Peugeot
75, Avenue de la Grande Armée
75116 PARIS
France

Dear Sir,

I am proud to own Peugeot 406 Estate – the perfect car for a family of four, plus two ageing (and it must be said rather smelly) Cocker Spaniels. I got it a few years ago, it's done about 90,000 miles and had a few bashes, but generally it's in reasonable shape.

As a driver, I am very interested in car advertising on television in the UK. In fact, there seems to be nothing but car advertising these days. This must make it hard for people to remember which car is being advertised. Particularly when all the adverts seem to follow the same formula: someone driving around in the car.

A chap I know who works in marketing told me the other day that these adverts cost a fortune: often more than the car itself. A lot of that money goes to the actors, and all they do is drive around in the cars. Then it occurred to me. These adverts don't get seen by many people; only those who are watching telly when they're on. Also, these people probably see other ads for Renault and Mazda and BMW. So you're paying these actors a lot of money to ride around in a Peugeot that won't be seen or remembered by many people. But I ride around in a Peugeot all the time. And I bet I'm seen by many more people. Yet I'm not getting any money from you at all. I don't think that's fair, do you?

Here I am – a living advertisement for your car every day of the year – and not getting a penny piece for it. Now I'm not a greedy man, but I do think I deserve some sort of remuneration. So I'm enclosing an invoice, backdated to when I bought the car and calculated till this June. I will not ask for any fees beyond June since I am likely to be trading in the Peugeot then for something smaller and more sensible.

I realise that sometimes in your adverts the actors drive around in more exotic locations like the highlands of Scotland or the French Riviera. Naturally I would be happy to oblige, but understandably this would incur a further fee, since I would either have to take the whole family plus dogs with me, or leave them at home – without the car.

I look forward to hearing from you with payment, shortly.

Bob Johnstone
Bob Johnstone.

P.S. It occurs to me that if you want to make an advert of me driving around, I could teach Dierdre how to use our video camera. It's quite a good one. That would be extra, though.

Sales Invoice

Invoice No: BOB 015

Date: _____

From: "Treetops" Spitfire Close, South Croydon, Surrey

Qty	Description	Amount exclusive of V.A.T. £	V.A.T. Net £
	Acting in a living advertisement for Peugeot 406 Estate as I drive around every day		
	Actor's fee per day: £25		
	3 years (July 2002 – June 2005) @ £50 per day		
	TOTAL: £27,375.00*		
	*This total may be paid in Euros or Sterling		
	Cheques payable to Bob Johnstone		
		Sub total exc. V.A.T. £	
		V.A.T. £	
		Total due £	

V.A.T. rate............................
Payment terms........................
Tax Point ....

DMQ/CPP
05.0071/DR/DG

Bob Johnstone
Treetops
58 Spitfire Close
South Croydon
Surrey

PARIS, 20 April

Dear Sir,

Thank you for your letter and your loyalty, but we can not, as your understand, give you anything for that .

Sincerely,

Didier RICHARD
Marketing, Quality Division
Advertising and Promotion

"TREETOPS", 58 SPITFIRE CLOSE, SOUTH CROYDON, SURREY

Didier Richard
Marketing, Quality Division
Advertising and Promotion
Automobiles Peugeot
75, Avenue de la Grande-Armée
75016 PARIS
France

Dear Didier,

How intriguing that your surname is also a first name! There are of course, a number of others who share this name. I wonder if you are related by any chance to Keith Richard of the Rolling Stones, or Cliff Richard – or perhaps even Little Richard? I myself once appeared as a spear carrier in the Chipstead Players production of Shakespeare's *Richard III*.

Anyway. many thanks for your reply. It's good to get a response to one's queries, however terse they may be and however difficult to understand. You say in your letter "as your understand", but I am afraid I do not understand at all. I sense that we may be miscommunicating because of the language barrier that separates our two great nations; a barrier much bigger than the English Channel itself, or La Manche as I believe you call it.

So in an attempt to communicate more effectively, I have asked my son Tristan to translate the rest of this letter into French, he is nearly 7 years old.

Cher Didier

Je ne vous demande pas de me donner l'argent pour ma fidélité (bien qu'ayez-vous considéré un arrangement de récompense de fidélité ? Je pourrais vous aider avec cela.) Je demande simplement que vous me payez sur votre budget de la publicité annoncer votre voiture là où que je vais. Pensez ce que cela vous coûterait d'avoir Peugeot annoncer en le R-U 24 heures sur 24, 7 jours par semaine et 365 jours de l'année - une fortune. Je ne pense pas donc que les honoraires que je demande sont l'issue. Est-elle parce que je suis britannique ? Je détesterais pour penser que n'importe quelle xénophobie existe chez Peugeot.

I do hope to hear from you with more positive news. If you find it difficult to write in English, please feel free to use your native tongue and I will get Tristan to translate.

Yours sincerely

Bob Johnstone

Bob Johnstone

"Cookeswithin"
99, Kerching Drive
Twickenham, Middx, UK

Penfolds
North American Office
2700 Napa Valley Corporate Drive
Suite A
Napa, CA 94558
USA

2nd April

Dear Sir or Madam,

I am a keen wine amateur, enjoying the process of wine growing as well as the drinking of it! As you are well aware, English wine is being taken more seriously than ever, with a variety of sparkling wines from vineyards such as Chapel Down and Ridge View holding their own in blind lineups which include many of the top French Champagnes. The best South of England vineyards are growing at an incredible rate of up to approximately 39% per year, but it is rumoured that they simply can't get enough grapes. I have, according to my gardener, the perfect chalk soil essential for growing the high-acidity white grapes required for sparking wine. And now with the introduction of global warming, we have something that could be very exciting here in the United Kingdom, as I'm sure you will agree.

What I am proposing is this: I would like to rent to you a small area of my garden to plant a few Vines in order to produce some grapes. This would eventually go towards producing a new local Sparkling Wine. I would have probably enough room for at least three vines initially, and I'm sure I could encourage our neighbours to participate in this "New world meets Old" project. I am currently working with another colleague living in Croydon who would also like to be involved in my little venture. He has an interesting south facing slope to the left of his garage that would suit the Pinot Noir and Chardonnay variety.

Imagine *"Croydon Creek"*, and *"Twickenham Ridge"* being available on the shelves of the local shops. Exciting or what? Or how about *"Old World Pommy-agnee?"* (Not to be confused with the cheap headache inducing pear fizz popular in the 70s.) We both have decent sized cellars that could easily give the Vintage a Cava status, and we could also hire from one of the theatrical accessory suppliers, a cobweb and dust machine that would add a certain aesthetic maturity to the bottles.

I have therefore enclosed an Invoice for your inspection that itemizes the specific cost for rent of garden space, and general upkeep of the vines, as well as costs for suggested branding and use of local names. I trust that you will enjoy considering this marvelous idea and I look forward to receiving your comments and thoughts in due course.

Kindest Regards and "Cheers!"

Bob Howard

Bob Howard

Sales Invoice

Date: _____ Invoice No: _____

From: "Cookeswithin" 99, Kerching Drive,
Twickenham, Middx, UK

Qty	Description	Amount exclusive of V.A.T. £	V.A.T. Net £
	Rent of garden space, roughly 6ft x 4 ft. Per week	(£20.50p)	
	Initial suggestion of both Twickenham and Croydon Vines special price per month	£99.99p	
	Upkeep, pruning, compost, watering system (Large watering can?)	£17.56p	
	Branding of local place names (10% of which would be paid to the appropriate local authorities as a gesture of goodwill)	£12.65p	
	Total price payable per month	£117.55p	
	I would suggest that both wines would be sold At around £11.98p upwards to attract the better More discerning wine drinker. If Cliff Richard can do it with Vida Nova I'm sure we can!		
		Sub total exc. V.A.T.£	
		V.A.T.£	
		Total due£	

V.A.T. rate............................
Payment terms......................
Tax Point..............................

April 6

Mr. Howard
Cookeswithin
99 Kerching Drive
Twickenham, Middx

Dear Mr. Howard:

Thank you for taking the time to contact us at Penfolds Winery.

All of us at Penfolds appreciates that you have considered our winery to be a part of your venture in grape growing and grape sourcing. However, we must decline your proposal.

We wish you all the best with your venture.

Please do not hesitate to contact me if you have any further queries or comments regarding Penfolds Winery or our products.

With kindest regards,

Vida V. Harris
Consumer Relations Manager

Enclosure

"Cookeswithin"
99, Kerching Drive
Twickenham, Middx, UK

Vida V. Harris
Penfolds
North American Office
2700 Napa Valley Corporate Drive
Suite A
Napa, CA 94558
USA

19th April

Dear Vida,

Thank you for your letter dated 6th April that also included the very generous gifts of a bottle opener and two non-drip pourers. I will pass on one of the non-drip pourers to my colleague in Croydon, who I know will be delighted.

I am sorry that you don't want to take up our offer of new vineyards in Twickenham and Croydon. I thought that Penfold would see the great advantages of establishing an exciting business in consumer marketing and new vineyard growth.

But looking on the bright side, I am coming over to California in the next couple of weeks, and wondered if I could pop in and say "Hello", and thank you personally for my lovely gifts? It's always good to put a face to the name, don't you agree?

Also, I could pick up a couple of Penfold vine cuttings that I could bring home and plant in my garden to see if they take in my chalky soil. If you could spare say four individual ones I could then give a couple to my friend in Croydon to see if they take down there on his Southerly Slope.

Please let me know if this would be convenient and when would be the best time to call. Maybe early afternoon so that I could sample a little of what's on offer?

Thank you again and I look forward to hearing from you and hopefully meeting up.

Kind Regards

Yours sincerely

Bob Howard

Bob Howard.

July 27th

Mr B Howard
"Cookeswithin"
99 Kerching Drive
Twickenham, Middx

Dear Mr Howard

Thank you for contacting us at Penfolds. We were most concerned to learn that you have not received any communication from us, regarding the letters you had previously sent.

To help me assist you further, I would be grateful if you could contact me on 0208 917 4687, to enable me to deal with this matter promptly.

Once again I apologise for the delay you have experienced and hope I will be able to sort out this matter very shortly.

Yours sincerely

Caroline Brooks
Events & Consumer Relations Coordinator

FGL WINE ESTATES EMEA   **CONSUMER LED & CUSTOMER DRIVEN**

Southcorp Wines Europe Limited (Subsidiary of Foster's Group Limited)
Grange House, 15 Church Street, Twickenham, Middlesex TW1 3NL United Kingdom Tel +44 (0)20 8917 4600 Fax +44 (0)20 8917 4646
VAT 668064412 Registered Company No.02808255 www.fglwineestates.com

"Cookeswithin"
99, Kerching Drive
Twickenham, Middx, UK.

Caroline Brooks,
Penfolds,
Southcorp Wines
Grange House,
15 Church Street,
Twickenham
TW1 3NL

1st August

Dear Caroline,

How totally amazing to hear from you.

I too have been concerned that despite three letters to you over a period of four months, I've heard absolutely nothing.

I have received a lovely reply from Vida V. Harris in Napa California, but even she didn't feel the need to reply to my second letter when I offered to *"Call in and say Hi!"* when I was recently visiting USA. Strange or what?

With regard to your letter and request to telephone you, I'm sure that you will understand that this wouldn't be the best option under the circumstances. You see, I prefer to write letters as it allows clarity of thought and prevents loose words being said and vague promises being offered.

I still feel that *"Croydon Creek"* and *"Twickenham Ridge"* would be a marvelous brand to develop but since writing to you, my "Partner in Wine" has moved to Riddlesdown, so perhaps his amended vintage could be *"Riddle's Puddle"*. It has a certain English charm don't you think?

Your letter is quite vague and suggests that you will be able to *"sort out this matter very shortly"*. I'm not sure what needs sorting. Either you like my ideas or you don't. It's as simple as that. I just want to know what you think.

I hope that I don't have to wait another four months for a reply.

Kind Regards,

Sincerely

Bob Howard

Bob Howard

"Cookeswithin"
99, Kerching Drive
Twickenham, Middx, UK

Leroy Jenkins
PO BOX 4270
Scottsdale
Arizona 85261
USA

11th May

Dear Leroy,

I was in New York recently and I was staying in one of the cities finest Hotels downtown. But suffering as I do from incurable jet lag, I found myself wide-awake at around 2am wondering what to do. The Gym was closed, as were all the shops, and the only option appeared to be my hotel room TV. That's when I saw you.

I was introduced to the phenomenon known as *Miracle Spring Water*. So simple and yet so perfect. I immediately wanted to order some there and then. It may well have helped me get back to sleep, who knows? Are people really healed through taking this water? Please tell me, honestly. No matter, it started me thinking about my idea. For some time I have wanted to market and distribute my *Healing through Herbs* concept. I believe that as with your *Miracle Spring Water*, there is a tangible and scientifically proven formula that offers hope, healing, wealth and forgiveness of sins through herbs. I know this sounds rather heretical and perhaps a little simplistic, but I can assure you that I am coming to this from a very strong evangelical and scriptural background. As you know there are many references in the Bible to spices, herbs and natural produce, both in the Old and New Testament.

So how about we go into business together? I would love to develop my HTH concept further and feel that there is a natural bond between us. Might I suggest Coriander for Colds? Fennel for Fever? Rosemary for Rheumatism? Dill for Diarrhoea? The list is endless. This could solve 95% of the worlds health problems in one shot, I'm sure you can see the amazing potential both here in USA and in the Western world.

So I am willing to offer you a share in this potentially vast empire of *Healing though Herbs* at an incredibly reduced introductory offer. Should you be interested in helping to market and distribute these miraculous and life changing produce, I will send you an introductory pack of all of my products including the scientifically tested *"How to keep you marriage alive using Oregano and Basil"*. It really does work. I've tested it personally! Please let me know how you would like to proceed and how soon I can send you some samples.

Warm Christian Greetings

Bob Howard

Sales Invoice

Date: _____ Invoice No: _____

From: "Cookeswithin" 99, Kerching Drive,
Twickenham, Middx, UK

Qty	Description	Amount exclusive of V.A.T. £	V.A.T. Net £
	Healing through Herbs Instruction book and Selection of specific courses. Choice of fifteen. Per Item		£76.99p
	Practical Video Guide: NTSC and PAL formats		£130.00p
	Sample of herb bed mini-pack, one month Complimentary supply.		£16.79p
	Grow your own window boxes for ongoing Benefit of Healing with herbs		£32.67p
	Mulch and specially formulated organic Manure with ingredient X (1 bag)		£18.99p
	Other costs available on request.		
	We do include Marijuana as one of our herbs containing very Specific medicinal properties but appreciate the delicate nature of Advertising this to a target market. Maybe you could suggest ways we could get round any difficult or ethical issues here? We also tithe our profits, as I'm sure you do too.		
		Sub total exc. V.A.T. £	
		V.A.T. £	
		Total due £	

V.A.T. rate.........................
Payment terms.........................
Tax Point.........................

THE LEROY JENKINS EVANGELISTIC ASSN., INC.
P.O. BOX 4270, SCOTTSDALE, AZ. 85261
Phone 480-609-9023

July 11

Dear Bob

Ihave always believed in the curative power of herbs. I don't know how we would do this. Let me know more about it.

Rev Jenkins

"Cookeswithin"
99, Kerching Drive
Twickenham, Middx, UK.

The Leroy Jenkins Evangelistic Assn., Inc.
PO BOX 4270
Scottsdale
Arizona 85261
USA

1st August

Dear Leroy,

Thank you for your exceptionally brief letter dated 11th July.

I was intrigued by your *Miracle Spring Water* and had the idea that along with my herbal experience, we could market together some additional brands that would appeal to your ever-growing market of sick people. How about mixing the two together? Using your water and my herbal mixtures, we could create a new line of healing accessories.

St. John's Wort with Miracle water.	This would treat depression.
Artichoke leaf and Miracle water.	Great for Irritable Bowel Syndrome.
Garlic and Miracle water.	Lowers cholesterol.
Mint and Parsley with Miracle water.	Clears Bad Breath from the garlic!

Should I send you a few mixtures for you to see where I'm coming from?

I wouldn't mind getting some of your Miracle water so I too could try to make a few blends. Could you send me a bottle?

Finally, just one question: do you still have your own hair? I'm losing mine and trying to find an herbal mixture that would help restore my locks to their former glory. Maybe the miracle water would help?

Kind regards

Bob Howard

Bob Howard

"One of them went out into the fields to gather **herbs** and found a wild vine. He gathered some of its gourds and filled the fold of his cloak. When he returned, he cut them up into the pot of stew, though no one knew what they were"... Deep eh?

LEROY JENKINS
EVANGELISTIC ASSOCIATION, INC.
PO BOX 4270
SCOTTSDALE, AZ 85261
OFFICE (480) 609-9023

Dear Partner in Christ;

It was great to hear from you today. Please find enclosed the material you requested. I have also enclosed some important information about our ministry.

God bless you, I will look forward to hearing from you again. Let me know your needs and, like a true partner should, I will join you in praying for those needs to be met, in Jesus' name, Amen.

Your friend and Evangelist,

Leroy Jenkins

BOOKS, TAPES & CD

ALL FOR A LOVE OFFERING

LEROY JENKINS EVANGELISTIC, ASSO
PO BOX 4270, SCOTTSDALE, AZ 85261
OFFICE 480-609-9023

Order Form For Books & Tapes

Name _____
Address _____
_____
City _____ State _____
Zip _____

Master Card / Visa

-- -- -- -- -- -- -- -- -- -- -- --

Exp Date __ __ - __ __
Signature _____

ITEM	QTY	PRICE

Anointed Water Instructions

Faith is the key. Obedience is the secret. I could go on and on, but just use this water as you feel God wants you to, and I believe God will heal you.

- Drink the Water
- Anoint Yourself
- Anoint your Home
- Anoint your Car
- Anoint any Article
- Pour it on a Burn
- Pour it on Sores
- Pour it where you have pain
- Touch your Wallet or Purse for a financial blessing.

OFFICE LOCATION
SCOTTSDALE, ARIZONA

PO BOX 4270
SCOTTSDALE
ARIZONA, 85261

OFFICE # 480-609-9023
PRAYERLINE # 480-609-9029

HEALING WATERS CHURCH

EVERY SUNDAY @ 11:30 AM
REV BOB FRARY
THE HAMILTON PLAZA HOTEL
2124 S HAMILTON RD
COLUMBUS, OH 43232

ANOINTED WATER

24-20 oz Bottles
$100 DONATION
NO SPLIT SHIPMENTS
NO P.O. BOX
STREET ADDRESS ONLY
US CONTINENT ONLY

CHECK OUT REVIVAL OF AMERICA ON
www.leroyjenkins.com

"Cookeswithin"
99, Kerching Drive
Twickenham, Middx, UK

Leroy Jenkins
PO BOX 4270
Scottsdale
Arizona 85261
USA

16th November

Dear Rev Jenkins,

Thank you for the Miracle Spring water that arrived recently. I was impressed at the delicate and yet space saving packaging, that discretely resembles a mini bottle. I was also intrigued at the information that came with the Miracle water and where you suggested I could sprinkle it. My eyes were immediately drawn to the option of anointing my wallet. So I decided to go the whole way; I took out my wallet and carefully placed it onto a sort of symbolic altar. I then placed a £5 note inside the wallet and on the note scribbled the specific amount that I would like to receive. Then I anointed my wallet with all three of the Miracle Spring water sachets you sent, and retired for the night.

In the morning I rushed downstairs to my makeshift shrine where I had left my wallet. Imagine my surprise when I discovered that nothing had happened! The £5 was still there, and there was absolutely no evidence of the £10,000.00p I had asked for. So I am asking you to help me again. I was banking on this money being there so I have to resort to other means. I am a firm believer in the Tithe so I have attached an Invoice for £1,000 by way of 10% of the expected total.

Please let me know how you would like to proceed with this, and your specific comments as to why this didn't work. The £1,000 will go towards my work of *Healing through Herbs* which I detailed to you previously.

Thank you, and although I am disappointed, I still think that we can work together.

I remain yours very sincerely

Bob Howard

Bob Howard

Sales Invoice

Date: _____ Invoice No: _____
From: _____

Qty	Description	Amount exclusive of V.A.T. £	V.A.T. Net £
	10% of expected miracle: "Anointing your wallet" as instructed in brochure		
	Total payable	£1000.00p	
	Of course I would be more than happy to use this as an advance against specific merchandising that I could send you through my "Healing through Herbs" ministry. You decide.		

"Cookeswithin"
99, Kerching Drive
Twickenham, Middx, UK

British Organ Donor Society,
BODY,
Balsham,
Cambridge,
CB1 6DL.

13th August

Dear Body,

I have some very fine organs. My heart, kidneys, liver, and lungs are all in tip-top condition. I use my ears professionally and my eyes see beyond twenty-twenty. My reproductive organ is second only to the Old Testament Patriarchs, and my brain is hopefully getting better, bigger, wiser, fuller and more mature as I progress through the years.

OK so why the letter? Well, I'm suggesting a move away from the rather illogical procedures of donating my organs, and instead, offering you all of the above for a specific fee. Why shouldn't I benefit from this now? If you agree to pay me for my organs, I will promise to care for them even more than I am doing at the moment.

I will further undertake to get annual examinations, and guarantee that my diet, and supplements will follow specific guidelines as suggested by you, and my doctor.

I am presently a vegetarian and haven't eaten red meat for thirty years. I don't drink alcohol (in excess anyway). I'm off dairy, wheat, and chips and I eat fruit and vegetables like an elephant.

I have enclosed an invoice of charges for my specific organs, and should you agree, I would be happy to accept a down payment as a gesture of goodwill.

What do you think? I guess I'd be happy for my heirs to receive any funds payable at a later stage, but it strikes me as silly not to take full advantage now of what is actually mine, as well as using it as an incentive to live better and have a healthier lifestyle.

So that's it. How do you feel about this? I know that my wife and my children would also be happy to be part of this new scheme, and of course, I'd do a special deal for a "job lot" so to speak!

I hope you find this idea of interest and that it may begin a new chapter in organ donations (for a fee) for BODY.*

I look forward with great interest to your reply.

Yours sincerely

Bob Howard

Sales Invoice

Date: _____ Invoice No: _____

From: "Cookewithin" 99, Kerching Drive,
Twickenham, Middx, UK

Qty	Description	Amount exclusive of V.A.T. £	V.A.T. Net £
	Organs For sale. To Include:	£1,000.00p	
	Heart	£1,000.00p	
	Liver	£750.00p	
	Kidneys. Each	£2,000.00p	
	Lungs	£1,500.00p	
	Penis and testicles (inc)	£5,000.00p	
	Brain and attached matter	£800.00p	
	Eyes, ears, nose, teeth, etc etc		
	Remainder of organs negotiable as per requested.		
	* Instead of BODY it would be BODFAFS (British Organ Donations For a Fee Society). Sounds like a small village in Wales doesn't it?		
		Sub total exc. V.A.T. £	
		V.A.T. £	
		Total due £	

V.A.T. rate _____
Payment terms _____
Tax Point _____

BODY
BRITISH ORGAN DONOR SOCIETY
REGISTERED CHARITY No 294925

BODY, Balsham, Cambridge CB1 6DL.
Tel: 01223 893636   Email: body@argonet.co.uk   Website: http://www.argonet.co.uk/body

---

Dear Mr Howard,

I apologise for not answering your letters - we are a small voluntary Charity run basically by two people.

What you are proposing is both **illegal and impractical**. The Human Tissue Act 2004 emphatically makes it illegal both to sell or offer to sell any organ or tissue.

You wish to receive a 'down' payment now! **Only a very few people are able to be donors at their death** - about one in 900. Most donors are brain stem dead on a ventilator - some kidneys can be removed from heart dead donors but it is a case of being in the right place at the right time. Who would pay for your and other 'hopefuls' organs - certainly not a small charity concentrating on support and information.

Lastly many of the items you offer for sale are not at present transplanted nor do I know of any future plans.

If you would like your organs to help someone sign up on the NHS Organ Donor Register to **donate** organs.

Yours faithfully

Margaret Evans
Margaret Evans

"Cookeswithin"
99, Kerching Drive
Twickenham, Middx, UK

Margaret Evans
British Organ Donor Society,
BODY,
Balsham,
Cambridge,
CB1 6DL.

30th October

Dear Ms. Evans,

Thank you from the bottom of my heart for your undated reply to my letters.

I can see that I have offended and upset you. This was unintentional. I was simply trying to offer you something that, for many years, I have looked after physically. I thought that it was a completely logical step to offer you my organs while I'm still around, live and kicking, rather than wait for the day when I don't need them any more. My mistake.

Would you be able to suggest anyone else who would appreciate my offer? Can you give me any details on the NHS Organ Donor Register? I can find no details on this anywhere.

I am also intrigued about your reference to The Human Tissue Act 2004 and would appreciate further clarification on the general matter of selling organs. Does this apply overseas as well?

Sorry to pester you again but I would like to know the answers to my questions, however silly you may think they are.

Thank you in advance,

Yours Organically,

Bob Howard
Bob Howard

BODY

BRITISH ORGAN DONOR SOCIETY
REGISTERED CHARITY No 294925

BODY, Balsham, Cambridge CB1 6DL.
Tel: 01223 893636   Email: body@argonet.co.uk   Website: http://www.argonet.co.uk/body

Dear Mr Howard,

Thank you for your letter. I am pleased you would like to sign up on the Organ Donor Register and enclose the relevant form which you can send Freepost.

I am so sorry to have been so long answering. We are basically a two man band and were away for a week at a Conference (and a few snatched days holiday) and on my return my monitor packed up leaving me computerless. Incidentally we weren't at all 'offended ' at your letter - I was just giving you the facts.

Yours sincerely

Margaret Evans
Administrator

"Cookeswithin"
99, Kerching Drive
Twickenham, Middx, UK

Waitrose Customer Service Department
Waitrose Limited
Doncastle Road
Bracknell
Berkshire
RG12 8YA

12th April

Dear Customer Services,

I have been a long-term supporter of Waitrose for many years, and try to encourage others to shop there. Having gone through the usual "cheap is best" way of shopping, I have now become an Organic Evangelist, seeking out all that is healthy, natural, low in fat and sugar, and non-processed. However, there appears to be a serious lack of really good quality chutneys, jams, spreads, and soups that give customers a full choice of flavours, and leaves you felling slightly disappointed when browsing the organic shelves at Waitrose

So I am writing to you is to see if you would be interested in taking my home made chutneys, jams and soups, to sell in your stores? Everyone who tries them tells me that they should be in the shops. I have managed to produce several recipes and never seem to have any left over after a batch of cooking and bottling them.

They're called "Howard's Good Old fashioned home made Extraordinarily Unusual Chutney / Jam / Soup". And recently I have been experimenting with a combination of produce that I feel work well together. My Apricot and Kipper Chutney is a favourite with the family as is my Banana and Turnip Jam with extra beef. The soups are also exciting with my Tripe and Brie Surprise being a real winner (The surprise is that I put a fish head at the bottom for extra flavour!) It's delicious.

I would be more than happy to send you some samples of my exciting range of produce, and I have also attached an invoice should you decide that you would like to purchase a batch for Waitrose. It would be good to find out exactly how many units you would ideally like for each store; I presently have only one assistant who works with me every other afternoon, and sometimes on a Saturday, so I would need to plan ahead.

I hope you will be interested in this new line for your stores, and as soon as you settle the invoice enclosed, I'll start sending them out to you. Thank you for reading this and I look forward to hearing from you as soon as possible.

Yours truly,

Roberta Howard (Mrs)

Roberta Howard (Mrs)

Sales Invoice

Date: _____ Invoice No: _____

From: "Cookeswithin" 99, Kerching Drive,
Twickenham, Middx, UK

Qty	Description	Amount exclusive of V.A.T. £	V.A.T. Net £
	Howard's Good Old fashioned home made Extraordinarily Unusual Chutney 435g* jars selection:		£14.99p
	Apricot & Kipper Chutney (box of 10 jars)		£13.87p
	Cheese omelette with raisins chutney.		£15.66p
	Sardine & Grapefruit chutney.		
	Jams:		
	Banana & Turnip jam with extra beef. (in units of three)		£6.00p
	Rhubarb and Fennel jam		£6.00p
	Left-overs with extra Syrup jam.		£5.22p
	Soups:		
	Tripe & Brie-fish-head surprise soup, (each)		£1.25
	Parsnip & Chocolate soup		£1.45
	Egg, bacon, & sausage soup		£1.65
	(*larger than the usual 335g to accommodate the long name)		
		Sub total exc. V.A.T £	
		V.A.T £	
		Total due £	

V.A.T. rate............................
Payment terms......................
Tax Point............................

ps. I decided to come to you first rather than approach Sainsburys Tesco or Asda. I hope you appreciate that?

Waitrose

Mrs Howard
Cookeswithin
99 Kerching Drive
Twickenham, Middx

25 April
1-5072677-7

Dear Mrs Howard

Thank you very much for your letter of 12 April concerning your suggestions for new and innovative chutneys, jams and spreads.

I have taken this opportunity to pass a copy of your correspondence to the relevant buyers. At this stage, we are not looking to increase our range or chutneys, jams and spreads. However, I would like to thank you for your time and effort and wish you success with your recipe's.

I can assure you of our commitment to providing the high standard of merchandise that you rightfully expect and deserve when shopping with us, and it remains my hope that you will continue to enjoy shopping with Waitrose. Should you have any other concerns please let me know at Waitrose Customer Service on 0800 188884.

Yours sincerely

Keith Brooks
Customer Service

900 H/O

Food shops of the John Lewis Partnership

Customer Service

Bracknell, Berkshire RG12 8YA
Telephone 01344 825232
Facsimile 01344 824978
email customer_service@waitrose.co.uk
www.waitrose.com

"Cookeswithin"
99, Kerching Drive
Twickenham, Middx, UK

Mr. Keith Brooks
Waitrose Customer Service Department
Waitrose Limited
Doncastle Road
Bracknell
Berkshire
RG12 8YA

17th May

Dear Keith,

How splendid to have your name behind that rather official title of WCSD.

My son's name was Keith. I have been tempted many times to name one of my spreads after him; Keith jam with extra pith. Do you think this would work?

Thank you for your kind letter dated 25th April; I would be more than interested in contacting your relevant buyers directly if possible. I'm certain that they would be interested in taking on some of my new and unique jam and chutney flavours.

Since receiving your encouraging news, I have decided to branch out and include breads, and cakes into my product line. Would you like me to send you a few samples of these?

I know it may sound bizarre, but due to the rather epidemic nature of the pigeon and squirrel population in Twickenham, I have taken to including them in my recipes: my Wholemeal Organic Loaf includes chunks of succulent pigeon breast. And my Squirrel Cookies with extra bran are a particular favourite with the Women's Church Group every Monday.

Please be assured that they do not suffer at all, and their demise is quite painless. I feel that not only am I helping to clean up our neighbourhood from unwanted vermin, I am providing a valuable service that includes nutritious protein, all home-baked. I'm sure this is something Waitrose would endorse, don't you? Please let me know. It would be marvellous to take some good news back to my Ladies group, and perhaps, you could come over one Monday lunchtime, and talk about your job in Customer Services? What a treat that would be.

Kindest Regards

Yours sincerely

Roberta Howard (Mrs)

Roberta Howard (Mrs)

Mrs Howard
Cookeswithin
99 Kerching Drive
Twickenham, Middx

19 May
1-5072677-7

Dear Mrs Howard

Thank you very much for your letter of 17 May. It is always a joy to receive correspondence from such a committed epicurean and reading about your range of game enhanced bread and cakes left me in doubt as to your deep commitment to your products.

I was of course very interested to learn that your son's name was Keith. Given that you refer to him in the past tense am I right in assuming that he is no longer with us, or that he has changed his name? Either way, if you are serious about marketing your spreads to a wider audience I would advise that you take the pith out of them first.

At Waitrose, we pride ourselves on offering a wide range of high quality products, and our buying team are charged with the challenge of developing new lines to meet the ever growing demand of our customers. I must admit, however, that the Squirrel Cookie eating denizens of your Women's Church Group are somewhat ahead of the zeitgeist in this regard, but I thought you would be interested to learn that there are a number of web sites that feature a range of squirrel recipes including www.scarysquirrel.org/recipes/ which you might like to access in order to get in touch with others with interests similar to your own.

I really appreciate your kind offer to talk to your ladies group about my role in Waitrose Customer Service. Please let me know what dates you have in mind. As before, I can be contacted on our freephone number 0800 188884.

Once again, thank you for taking the time to write, and updating me on your burgeoning food empire.

Yours sincerely

Keith Brooks
Customer Service

900 H/O

go to 5th avenue and
scrape squireel off pav
add onion, pepper, ga
fry in oil for 15 minut

ed Squirell by Cuzz
e yore daddy's
o skwerl huntin
gdom come!

scary squirrel world - recipes for cookin' up squirrel!!

Page 4 of 50

vegies are resisting being associated with this.) Str
large holed colander when meat has left bone and re
especially small ones. Return soup to the pot and add
leaves. Thicken with a little flour or gravox. Cut fried br
squares and serve soup over toast, boiling hot.

W. Hunter's Terriaki Squirrel

scary squirrel world - recipes for cookin' up squirrel!!

scary squirrel world

click pic for aunty frailty's suggestion

COOKIN' UP SKWERL

BURGOO FO

TYPE IN YOUR RECIPE; THEN CLICK ONCE;
YOU'LL BE SENT TO THE THANKS PAGE.

SEND

UNDO

NEW RECIPES

ood-related Sound #153   Food-related Sound #154   Food-related
Dawg Treets - anonymous   Sound #155

, blast 5 of them skally wags, pull off thier litt
guts, wash em, stick em in a fried pan, m
big pizza with eveything on that son
there skally wags to you doog.
mous

"Cookeswithin"
99, Kerching Drive
Twickenham, Middx, UK

Mr. Keith Brooks
Waitrose Customer Service Department
Waitrose Limited
Doncastle Road
Bracknell
Berkshire
RG12 8YA

15th June

Dear Keith,

What can I say? What an amazing and delightful bundle: 50 pages of Squirrel recipes no less. Thank you so very much. It was a great surprise not only to get your lovely letter offering to speak at our ladies group, but the inspiring and time-consuming pages of enlightening and mouth watering dishes left me speechless. Your copying machine must have been red hot! I wasn't sure if they were all meant to be taken seriously: Squirrel Squash, for example? Ingredients: one Squirrel, and a hammer.

From your response and recipes, you appear to be quite taken with the idea of using unconventional ingredients which is why I believe Waitrose would be a perfect partner to my "burgeoning food empire" as you have so jovially called it.

Please forgive the delay in my writing back to you but I have just returned from a trip to America. As part of our "Cooks Ahoy", we encourage our members to travel and experience different culinary dishes from around the world, and this time, I had the pleasure of spending two weeks on horseback, riding, sleeping, and eating *Au Naturel* (outdoors, not naked). Travelling around The Panhandle-plains in Texas, sleeping under the stars, and eating whatever was available, my eyes were well and truly opened. And of course I have returned with renewed vigour and inspiration.

Imagine if you will Skunk-burgers, Elkees spread (made from fresh Elk) Snake Chowder, Lizard Tongues On Crackers, Coyote Droppings with salsa, Rootworm Beetle Dip, and Desert Frog Croquettes. An almost endless list of extraordinary yet delicious dishes.

So my new "Howard's Healthy Fast Food selection" is about to be created. Why eat beef or ham when you can get such a variety of meats? Would this be something Waitrose would consider? I have now, with your help, been inspired to branch out further, and need to find a suitable outlet for my many ideas most of which you now are familiar with. Are there any branches in the UK who would take the risk? I know it would be an enormous success. How about somewhere a little "out of the way" to start with? Like Wymondham Norfolk or Willerby, East Riding of Yorkshire. Perfect places to experiment, and once successful, you could introduce the new range to London and the Home Counties. It's what happens in the theatre before a play comes into the West End, so why not the same with food?

Today, we have our ladies annual committee meeting where we plan our next years' activity. So hopefully I will be back to you with a few dates when you can come to speak about your many experiences with Waitrose.

Kind Regards and hopefully hear from you with some good news soon.

Yours sincerely,

Roberta Howard (Mrs)
Roberta Howard (Mrs.)

Mrs Howard
Cookeswithin
99 Kerching Drive
Twickenham, Middx

16 June
1-5072677-7

Dear Mrs Howard

Thank you so much for your letter of 15 June.

I was delighted to learn of your pleasure with the squirrel recipes I sent, and was struck by your palpable excitement about the 'extraordinary yet delicious dishes' you ate whilst traversing the Texas Panhandle.

I've never visited the area myself, but learning of your evident pleasure having made the trip, I'm very tempted to go. I wonder, could you tell me the way to Amarillo?

I'd like to wish you all the very best with 'Howard's Healthy Fast Food Selection', but as I mentioned in my previous letter, I think your product ideas are a little ahead of the zeitgeist for us; and that includes our more adventurous customers in Wymondham and Willerby.

I trust your ladies' annual committee meeting went well on the 15 June, and I look forward to learning the dates you have in mind when you would like me to come along to speak to your group. I'd be delighted to hear from you, and can be contacted on our freephone number 0800-188884.

Yours sincerely

Keith Brooks
Customer Service

900 H/O

Food shops of the John Lewis Partnership
Customer Service
Bracknell, Berkshire RG12 8YA
Telephone 01344 825232
Facsimile 01344 824978
email customer_service@waitrose.co.uk
www.waitrose.com

"Cookeswithin"
99, Kerching Drive
Twickenham, Middx, UK

Readers Digest Association
Customer services,
Leicester, LE55 8AA

26th February

Dear Sir,

I have been an avid supporter of *Readers Digest*, and was happy to receive one of your *Readers Digest* diaries last Christmas as a gift.

My work as a local vicar depends on accurate information in a diary, a church calendar, or any other form of appointment platform.

So having bravely got through Christmas, I highlighted Lent, Easter, Bank Holidays, Birthdays, High days and so on.

A week before 7th February, which was Shrove Tuesday, I began planning a special event for the church over-70s group. This was to be a large gathering to celebrate the start of Lent, and prepare our oldies for a period of what we call "fun-fasting". I purchased several dozen eggs, flour, gallons of milk, lemons, oranges, sugar, and a variety of sweet and savoury fillings.

By the time I had finished making roughly 300 pancakes, I was strangely conscious that no one had arrived. I couldn't think why. It had been announced and I had been told that people were looking forward to a time of food, fun and fellowship.

I made a call to one of my parishioners and was told that Shrove Tuesday was 28th February, and not 8th as it was clearly noted in your diary. What a gaff eh?

Mr Norris, my trusted chief warden offered to come over and help reduce my pancake mountain saying that he could probably manage around seventy in one sitting, but by then I had lost interest.

I'm planning to do this again on the correct day but sadly I can't use any of the original ingredients as they were all used up and the milk's gone off.

So I am attaching an invoice to cover costs for both the wrong date and the correct one in the hope that you will understand my pancake plight and rectify the mistake which was really your fault.

You will be pleased to hear that all other dates in your diary are correct.

I hope to hear from you soon.

Every Blessing,

Bob Howard

Rev Bob Howard

Sales Invoice

Date: _____ Invoice No: _____

From: "Cookeswithin" 99, Kerching Drive, Twickenham, Middx, UK

Qty	Description	Amount exclusive of V.A.T.£	V.A.T. Net £
	Purchase of 15 Dozen Eggs, Milk, Sugar, Plain flour, Lemons, Oranges, Syrup, Honey,	£38.76p	
	Fillings to include Jam, Tuna fish (cans) Mince meat, sardines, Diced carrots, Tomato soup, currants, milk chocolate, and Hundreds and Thousands.	£41.99p	
	Six bottles of sweet sherry and one bottle of Gin (for Mr. Norris)	£33.84p	
	I would of course be more than happy for this to go to a charity of your choosing so you don't think I'm "Out for the money" so to speak!		
		Sub total exc. V.A.T.£	
		V.A.T.£	
		Total due£	

V.A.T. rate............................
Payment terms......................
Tax Point ....

"Cookeswithin"
99, Kerching Drive
Twickenham, Middx, UK

Readers Digest Association
Managing Director
Customer services,
Leicester, LE55 8AA

6th October

Dear Sir,

I am somewhat baffled and disappointed. Despite my having written to you in February on a matter concerning your Diary and grave mistakes therein, I find myself prompted to write again to you in October to remind you that I have still not received a reply.

Is this the normal practice of *Readers Digest*?

The fault, that caused me originally to write to you, was indeed yours, and as you will see from the enclosed copy, it created distress, inconvenience and unnecessary expense.

I would value hearing from you as my parishioners have been asking if there had been any feedback, and possible compensation. Indeed Mr Norris has still sadly not completely recovered.

Please could you put this request into the hands of someone who would find the time, and have the courtesy to offer some reason why your diary was so misleading?

I expect a reply, and as a loyal customer of *Readers Digest*, politely demand one.

Yours most sincerely

Bob Howard

Rev. Bob Howard MA. BD (hons)

CUSTOMER SERVICES

18 October

Rev. B Howard
Cookeswithin
99 Kerching Drive
Twickenham, Middx

RXM//01416629

Dear Reverend Howard,

Thank you for your recent letter.

Unfortunately, I have not been able to trace your previous letter and so I am not sure what your enquiry is about. I would be grateful, therefore, if you could call us free on 0800 181151, quoting your Customer Number, and a member of our Customer Services Team will be able to deal with your query. Alternatively, you can write full details at the foot of this letter and return it to me in the enclosed reply-paid envelope.

I hope that I have been of assistance.

Yours sincerely

J Pether

p.p. Roxanne Wormleighton
Customer Relations Department

Encl. BRE

The Reader's Digest Association Limited, Leicester LE55 8AA.
Telephone Customer Service 08705 113366 www.readersdigest.co.uk

Registered Office The Reader's Digest Association Limited, 11 Westferry Circus Canary Wharf London E14 4HE
Registered Number 340452 England

7ABH

"Cookeswithin"
99, Kerching Drive
Twickenham, Middx, UK

Readers Digest Association
Customer services,
Leicester, LE55 8AA

28th October

Dear Mr/ Ms / Miss Pether

Thank you so very much for your reply to my letter, and please forgive the tardiness of my reply. I have been away in foreign parts as part of my ongoing ministry. I like to compare my professional activities to those of the effect of liquorice; *"Going into dark interiors and doing good works!"*

I do feel that humour is a great blessing, don't you? Where indeed would we be without a sense of humour, I ask you? Germany, most probably!

Anyway I seriously digress.

The reason for my initial contact with you was a matter of relative seriousness caused solely and exclusively by your *Readers Digest* Diary. In short, it detailed incorrect information that created confusion and culinary havoc over Lent. My first letter does explain the conundrum, which I have attached again.

As you will see, I was unable to write full details of this at the foot of your letter, as the details are quite long and, well, detailed. The font would have been miniscule, and, unless your eyesight is unbelievably good, you would have had great difficulty in making any sense of it.

I do however appreciate the reply-paid envelope which does help to relive an already cumbersome financial burden in my parish.

I was curious to see that you had copied in a Miss Roxanne Wormleighton. Is she any relation to Major General Grenville P Wormleighton, retired, who is one of my closest parishioners? Just curious that's all.

Anyway, I would be delighted to hear back from you; I remain confused about your diary, and perplexed that my letters have taken so long to reach a human being, but I feel assured and comforted that you may be able to shed some light on my initial problems, and draw this matter to a swift and happy conclusion.

I look forward to hearing from you soon.

Kind Regards

Yours sincerely

Bob Howard

Bob Howard Rev.

MANAGING DIRECTOR: ANDREW LYNAM-SMITH

29th November

Rev.B Howard
Cookeswithin
99 Kerching Drive
Twickenham, Middx

Dear Reverand Howard

Thank you for your letter of 28th October which has been passed to me by Mrs Pether.

I must apologise for the error in the Reader's Digest Diary, which I did now know about, but I regret that we cannot accept any liability for the cost of your event.

However, if you would like to nominate a charity, I would be pleased to make a donation of £100. A stamped addressed reply envelope is enclosed.

Yours sincerely

Andrew Lynam-Smith

"Cookeswithin"
99, Kerching Drive
Twickenham, Middx, UK

Mr. Andrew Lynam-Smith
Readers Digest Association
11 Westferry Circus
Canary Warf
London E14 4HE

18th December

Dear Mr Lynam-Smith,

Thank you for your letter dated 28th November. First I would like to apologize for the delay in writing back to you. As I'm sure you will appreciate, this is one of my busy periods, with Advent and Christmas greedily over-booking "rooms at the old Inn" if you get my religious drift?

I am personally relieved that your *Reader's Digest* diary managed to get the Christmas dates correct. We could have ended up *"A-Dinging and A-Donging Merrily"*, and *"Harking to those blessed Herald Angels"* sometime in early February! Mind blowing and excessively time consuming to say the least!

Before I address the main thrust and kind intent of your reply, I feel duty bound to put on my "alternative" hat, that of Deputy Headmaster and English tutor. So I am awarding your letter to me 10 out of 10 for generous content, but sadly, only 6 out of 10 for spelling and grammar. I would normally use the traditionally dreaded red pen and mark with unintelligible comments, but for now I'll explain simply, and neatly.

First, it's Reverend not Reverand, and the grammar in your sentence *"I must apologise for the error in The Reader's Digest Diary, which I did now know about"* simply makes no sense at all. (Copy Enc.) Maybe in your busy schedule you dictated your letter to one of your many secretaries, so I quite understand how these errors may have occurred. I will leave this now with a "Must try harder in future" and "Some room for improvement" (or perhaps get a new secretary?).

But now I feel duty bound to thank you most humbly for your kind and generous offer to donate £100 to my chosen Charity. This is very kind of you and I accept this lovely gesture. I would like to appoint The BBC Children in Need appeal for the £100 gift donation which I know will be gratefully received.

If there is any way you could keep me informed when this will happen, and I too will keep you posted on future events in the parish that hopefully won't be further confused by any errors in next year's *Reader's Digest* diary.

Thank you again, and I hope to hear from you soon with anything you wish to share with me, and my dedicated parishioners.

Yours most sincerely

Bob Howard
Rev Bob Howard

MANAGING DIRECTOR: ANDREW LYNAM-SMITH

21st December

Rev. B Howard
Cookeswithin
99 Kerching Drive
Twickenham, Middx

Dear Reverend Howard

Thank you for your letter of 18th December.

As requested, I am pleased to confirm that I have today sent a donation of £100 in favour of BBC Children in Need.

Yours sincerely

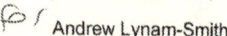

Andrew Lynam-Smith

"Cookeswithin"
99, Kerching Drive
Twickenham, Middx, UK

British Menopause Society
4-6 Eton Place,
Marlow,
Buckinghamshire.
UK SL7 2QA
10th June

Dear Sir or Madam,

Please forgive my informal introduction; I have never written to the British Menopause Society before and therefore I feel I have to tread somewhat delicately.

It is commonly known that Phytoestrogens, oestrogens isoflavones and lignans isoflavones are genistein and daidzein. The major lignans are enterolactone and enterodiol. The isoflavone daidzein is metabolized extensively in the gut by the human gut microflora to the more oestrogenic secondary metabolite equol. Herbs such as black cohosh, kava kava, evening primrose which is rich in gamma linolenic acid, dong quai, ginkgo biloba, ginseng, and equally important Steroids such as dehydroepiandrosterone, progesterone transdermal creams and the like, all contribute to alleviate this condition.

But how can you communicate that to the woman in the street, I ask you?

As you have probably gathered I have studied the subject of the Menopause for some time, and I have come to the conclusion that I can now help many women who suffer from this rather uncomfortable and inevitable condition.

I would like to introduce you to my new book: *"Women who Flush!"*

It's explains the effects of the menopause and how my new and original research and designs can help immediately stop the condition known as *"Women who Flush!"* But it doesn't stop there. Here comes the best bit:

The Flush-Jacket. This is a fully fitted designer jacket that is filled with crushed ice. Similar to a cooler that encases a bottle of wine, The Flush-jacket is stored in an ordinary freezer, and as soon as the hot flush begins, the jacket can be quickly taken from the freezer, and worn until the hot flush terminates. It's so easy, and it works.

I have designed the flush-jacket in three sizes, small, medium, and large, with a sporty modern finish in silver and black.

Amazingly, men can suffer from this condition too as you probably know (I certainly do!) and this Flush Jacket works a treat for them too.

I am sure that you will be interested in this innovative development and I have included an Invoice for the cost of the book and jacket so you can consider buying some to advertise on your website and anywhere else The British Menopause Society is active.

I would be more than happy to send you some examples and proofs, and obviously, the more you order, the cheaper they become.

Please let me know what you think of this as soon as possible, and hopefully we can join forces to help *"Women who Flush"*.

I look forward to your reply with excitement.

Yours sincerely

Bob Howard

Bob Howard

Sales Invoice

Date: _____ Invoice No: _____

From: "Cookeswithin" 99, Kerching Drive,
Twickenham, Middx, UK

Qty	Description	Amount exclusive of V.A.T. £	V.A.T. Net £
	"Women who Flush!". A new publication to combat The Menopause.		
	Book Publication		£17.99p
	Video (VHS Only)		£23.78p
	Audio Tape of Book (cassette)		£21.00p
	The Flush-Jacket (Women) S.M.L.		£199.89p
	The Flush-Jacket (Men) S.M.L.XXL.		£299.89p
	Additional ice pack refills. Per ten		£29.66p
		Sub total exc. V.A.T.£	
		V.A.T.£	
		Total due£	

V.A.T. rate ....
Payment terms ....
Tax Point ....

"Cookeswithin"
99, Kerching Drive
Twickenham, Middx, UK

British Menopause Society
4-6 Eton Place,
Marlow,
Buckinghamshire.
UK SL7 2QA

28th June

Dear Sir or Madam,

I was just wondering if you had received my letter dated 10th June?

I would be curious to find out what you thought of my ideas and creations that were carefully detailed in my letter. The main reason being the fact that I would like to approach BBC Woman's Hour with the news of my *Women who Flush* publication and *The Flush Jacket*, both of which I am certain would be of great interest to them. I have a direct line of contact with Jenny Murray so the sooner the better.

If you could find the time to get back to me with some thoughts and suggestions I would be very grateful.

Sorry to trouble you unnecessarily and I hope to hear from you with some encouraging news very soon.

Kind Regards

Yours sincerely

Bob Howard
Bob Howard

BRITISH MENOPAUSE SOCIETY

29th June

Bob Howard
Cookeswithin
99 Kerching Drive
Twickenham, Middx

Dear Sir

Thank you for your letter dated 28th June, which also attached your letter of 10th June.

May we apologise for the delay in responding to your letter, this is due to the fact that our annual conference is taking place next week in Torquay and as you can imagine this is creating a heavy workload and is taking priority.

Our next Council meeting is not until September but I shall bring your letters to the Council members' attention at that meeting. In the meantime, may we wish you well with your endeavours.

Yours faithfully

F A Patterson
Director

Chairman: Miss J. Pitkin BSc, FRCS, FRCOG
Chairman Elect: Professor J W. Studd MBChB, FRCOG, DSc
Hon. Treasurer: Mr A.M. Mander MBChB, FRCOG
Executive Director: Mr F.A. Patterson, MRIPHH, A.F.F.P, F.Inst.D
Deputy Director: Dr M.A. Upsdell MB, ChB, Dip Ven(Liverp)
4 - 6 Eton Place, Marlow, Bucks, SL7 2QA
Tel: 01628 890199 Fax: 01628 474042
E-mail: director.bms@btconnect.com or admin.bms@btconnect.com
Registered Charity No. 101544
Company Limited by Guarantee No. 2759439
Registered Office as above

"Cookeswithin"
99, Kerching Drive
Twickenham, Middx, UK

Mr. F A Patterson,
British Menopause Society
4-6 Eton Place,
Marlow,
Buckinghamshire.
UK SL7 2QA

4th July

Dear Mr. Patterson,

Thank you for your reply dated 29th June. Am I too late to attend the annual conference in Torquay? This is exactly the opportunity I would need to advertise and network my new ideas.

"*Woman who Flush!*" would attract a great deal of attention I know, and I could be personally demonstrated *The Flush Jacket* there and then at the conference. I could even set up a little stall at the Imperial Hotel where I have stayed many times. Would you be able to give some endorsement so that maybe on Thursday or Friday of this week I could pop down with a few copies of the book and some of my jackets? This is very exciting indeed.

I noted as well that your next Council Meeting is in September. Is there any chance of putting another "emergency meeting" in before that? I need to contact Jenny Murray at BBC Radio 4 as soon as possible and September may just be too late for me.

Let me know if you can accommodate me on this and I'm sure I can do some very special deals on my products.

Let me know also about this week and maybe we can have a chat over a beer about these exciting times.

I await your reply with great interest.

Yours sincerely

Bob Howard

Bob Howard

BRITISH MENOPAUSE SOCIETY
Meeting the Challenge of Menopause

14 July

Mr B Howard
Cookeswithin
99 Kerching Drive
Twickenham, Middx

Dear Mr Howard

Thank you for your letter dated 4th July regarding The Flush Jacket.

We regret that there is very little that we can do for you at the moment.

We are certainly unable to have an emergency meeting as our people come from all over the UK and as far as endorsement goes, we do not endorse any product of any description.

May we suggest that you go ahead with your contact with Jenny Murray and if interest is still around September 6th and 7th, when we will be holding our Annual Conference in Edinburgh, it may be possible for you to have a small table at our Exhibition, but as we have not yet had the opportunity of looking at Edinburgh in detail we will need to contact one another nearer those dates.

We hope that this is helpful to you.

Yours sincerely

F A Patterson
Director

Chairman: Professor J.W. Studd DSc, MBChB, FRCOG
Immediate Past Chairman: Miss J. Pitkin BSc, FRCS, FRCOG
Hon. Treasurer: Mr A.M. Mander MBChB, FRCOG
Executive Director: Mr F.A. Patterson, MRIPHH, A.F.F.P, F.Inst.D
Deputy Director: Dr M.A. Upsdell MB, ChB, Dip Ven(Liverp)
4 - 6 Eton Place, Marlow, Bucks, SL7 2QA
Tel: 01628 890199 Fax: 01628 474042
E-mail: director.bms@btconnect.com or admin.bms@btconnect.com
Registered Charity No. 1015144
Company Limited by Guarantee No. 2759439
Registered Office as above

"Cookeswithin"
99, Kerching Drive
Twickenham, Middx, UK

Mr. F A Patterson,
British Menopause Society
4-6 Eton Place,
Marlow,
Buckinghamshire.
UK SL7 2QA

26th July

Dear Mr. Patterson,

Thank you so much for your reply dated 14th July. I was excited at your suggestion to contact Jenny Murray at BBC Radio 4's Woman's Hour, but a little concerned about your Annual Conference date. Is it really September 2006 or was this a typing error? I can only assume it was. I'm not sure I can wait that long.

I was also thrilled to receive your encouraging words regarding *The Flush Jacket* and wanted you to be the first to know about *The "New" Flush Helmet* that is currently being tested in Beta form at the moment. It's a stand-alone hat but can also be used as an insert to alleviate flushing and embarrassing overheating slightly more discretely than the jacket. We are currently developing this with a well-known Bond Street milliners to add the necessary fashion status to our brand.

Thank you for the theoretical offer of a small table at the conference. Of course we can talk nearer the time, but due to the physical size of both the jackets and the helmets, not to mention the portable ice packs, I think that I will need something closer to a very large table simply to fit everything on. But we can discuss these details later.

Finally, may I congratulate you on your new headed paper. I personally prefer the recent blue design. The grey/beige was a little too austere and gloomy. I hope you don't mind my saying that?

I look forward to your clarifying the date of your Annual Conference and thought, if any, on the possible benefits as you see them of the New Flush Helmet.

Thank you again for your interest and encouragement,

With Kind Regards

Yours sincerely

Bob Howard

Bob Howard (Author of *Woman who Flush*)

"Cookeswithin"
99, Kerching Drive
Twickenham, Middx, UK.

British Airways Customer Relations (S506)
PO Box 5619
Sudbury
Suffolk
CO10 2PG

May 19th

Dear Customer Relations,

I am writing to you in a state of some confusion. Please allow me to explain.

I have been listening to your new radio campaign that advertises a variety of special offers throughout Europe. Whilst driving in the car, or listening to the radio at home, I specifically heard your commercials saying: *"British airways special offer to Prague – £71.00 including taxis."** So being the adventurous type, I booked my flight and flew to the lovely city of Prague. I collected by baggage and arrived at the taxi collection point outside the terminal. I climbed into the next available taxi and asked him to take me to Hotel Adria, Vaclavske namesti 26, which is in the centre of town.

When we arrived at the hotel I asked the driver about the British Airways special offer that clearly told me on the radio that my fare *"included all taxis"*. He didn't understand what I was saying, and eventually I found the Hotel Concierge who tried to translate for me. He was as confused as the taxi driver, and finally, to save time I paid the taxi fare, which was somewhere in the region of £50 plus a large tip. This presented me with a major problem. Due to your amazing offer of *"fares including taxis"*, I had planned to do all of my sightseeing of Prague in one of their local cabs. As there was no one I could call to confirm what I had initially understood, I decided to cut short my stay and come home. Where did I go wrong? What in fact was your offer?

Arriving back at Gatwick, I imagined that the problems I'd experienced in Prague could have been due to the language barrier and their possible dislike of tourists, so I attempted to negotiate again my *"all inclusive"* taxi back to Nuneaton, where I was staying with my sister. But the taxi driver refused to listen and charged me the unbelievable fare of £257.87p which was confirmed on his meter. Needless to say, he didn't get a tip! Apart from a rather short trip to Prague, I felt somehow misled, and confused. And of course seriously out of pocket. So I am sending you the attached invoice for taxi fares that I had heard were included in my trip to Prague, but clearly were not!

I would be interested to hear your side of the story and why I didn't get any taxi vouchers, and why the taxi drivers were unaware of your offer. I hope you can see this from my perspective and I look forward to hearing from you with an explanation.

Yours confusingly,

Bob Howard

(* Paraphrased version of what I heard, and not literally word for word, and I only mentioned Prague as it was somewhere I wanted to visit)

Qty	Description	Amount exclusive of V.A.T.
	Additional taxi fares previously thought to be included in the special offer fare price.	
	Taxi fares in Prague	£110.00p
	Taxi to Nuneaton	£257.87p
	Total payable	£367.87

(I took the train to the airport on the way to Gatwick which is why I haven't included that. I don't want you to think I'm taking advantage.)

BRITISH AIRWAYS

Customer Relations
PO Box 5619 (S506)
Sudbury Suffolk CO10 2PG UK
Tel 0870 850 9850
Tel +44 (0)191 490 7901
Fax +44 (0)20 8759 4314

16 June

Mr Bob Howard
Cookeswithin
99 Kerching Drive
Twickenham, Middx

Our Ref: 4198652

Dear Mr Howard

Thank you for your letter about our recent radio campaign.

The offer that you are referring to included the airfare, taxes, fees and charges. Because of this reason I am afraid I am unable to offer you a refund of the taxi fares you paid. Please accept my apologies if this offer caused you any confusion.

I know that this must be disappointing but I hope I have managed to explain the background. I hope you will fly with us again in the not too distant future.

Yours sincerely

Kelly Robson
Customer Relations

British Airways Plc
Registered Office: Waterside PO Box 365 Harmondsworth UB7 0GB
Registered in England No. 1777777

www.britishairways.com

"Cookeswithin"
99, Kerching Drive
Twickenham, Middx, UK.

Kelly Robson
British Airways Customer Relations (S506)
PO Box 5619
Sudbury
Suffolk
CO10 2PG

23rd June

Your Ref: 4198652

Dear Kelly,

Thank you so much for your letter dated 16th June. I am honoured that you have seen it necessary to give me a reference number that I'm sure means something to you. Or does this refer to the number of letters you have dealt with to date?

No matter, I think I have figured out what went wrong with my trip and subsequent expenses, and I feel a little foolish.

You see, when I heard the Radio commercials, I heard something to the effect of *"... Includes airfare, taxis, fees and charges ..."* And now as you have so patiently pointed out to me in your reply, it's NOT Taxis, but Taxes!!! How stupid can a person be? It's amazing how one letter in a word can change so much, and in my case, an entire holiday! Take *Flights*, and *Frights*, *Plane*, and *Plate*! Scary isn't it? Even changing one letter in both of your names you can end up with *Belly Rubson*. Sounds like a question they'd asked in a dodgy Scottish Massage Parlour! Banish the thought.

So can you see how this happened? You explained in perfectly in your letter, but I still managed to ruin my holiday through a simple case of mispronunciation. What would you suggest? I've heard of noise canceling headphones for flying, but I think I need some noise-enhancing ones. Do you know where I can get some?

I would love to fly again with British Airways but could do with some additional encouragement to do so. So any suggestions, confidential reassurances, or tempting vouchers would be gratefully received. And next time I get into a Taxi, I will hear your kind but firm words reminding me of the error of my ways.

I hope to hear from you again soon with something that may tease me back.

Kind Regards

Yours slightly less confused

Bob Howard

Bob Howard (or playing our little game again *"Boo-Ho-hard"*)

BRITISH AIRWAYS

Customer Relations
PO Box 5619 (S506)
Sudbury Suffolk CO10 2PG UK
Tel 0870 850 9850
Tel +44 (0)191 490 7901
Fax +44 (0)20 8759 4314

30 June

Mr Bob Howard
Cookeswithin
99 Kerching Drive
Twickenham, Middx

Our Ref: 4198652

Dear Mr Howard

Thank you for your letter of 23 June

I'm afraid I am unable to offer you any form of voucher for future travel with us. I know this will not be the news you hoped for.

I hope that this will not come as too much of a disappointment and that you'll be joining us on a British Airways flight again soon.

Yours sincerely

Kelly Robson
Customer Relations

British Airways Plc
Registered Office Waterside PO Box 365 Harmondsworth UB7 0GB
Registered in England No. 1777777

www.britishairways.com

"Cookeswithin"
99, Kerching Drive
Twickenham, Middx, UK.

Kelly Robson
British Airways Customer Relations (S506)
PO Box 5619
Sudbury
Suffolk
CO10 2PG

4th July

Your Ref: 4198652

Dear Kelly,

Thanks again for your briefest of notes dated 30th June.

I'm surprised that you haven't received similar mail from people being confused like I was. Have you received any other problems like this? Am I the only stupid, hard of hearing passenger that misheard *Taxes* for *Taxis*? Or maybe I'm the only one who's bothered to write? I don't know.

Having been to New York recently (with Virgin this time just in case you were wondering?) I noticed several of the large B.A. posters that dominate many of he buildings in Manhattan.

Maybe you should suggest they add one more? *"When we say including Taxes, we don't mean Taxis!"* You never know, it might just catch on. Should I send this to Saatchi and Saatchi's?

Let me know and I'll send them an invoice too.

Kind Regards

Yours hopefully

Bob Howard
Bob Howard

BRITISH AIRWAYS

Customer Relations
PO Box 5619 (S506)
Sudbury Suffolk CO10 2PG UK
Tel 0870 850 9850
Tel +44 (0)191 490 7901
Fax +44 (0)20 8759 4314

06 July

Mr Bob Howard
Cookeswithin
99 Kerching Drive
Twickenham, Middx

Our Ref: 4198652

Dear Mr Howard

Thank you for your letter.

I am concerned you are still unhappy with our explanation about the way we advertise our fares.

I am afraid there is nothing more I can add to our previous explanation. It is standard practise for the airline industry to advertise the fare and then advise if this fare includes taxes fees and charges. It is in fact a practise recommended by the Advertising Standards Authority.

I realise that you had planned your holiday around your understanding that all your taxis would be free of charge. We have looked carefully at the radio advertisement in question - it does state clearly taxes fees and charges. As you will appreciate we advertise worldwide and we have to be sure our advertising is clear and honest so we appreciate your comments.

As we have never received any similar complaints I am afraid this appears to have been a misunderstanding, so I am unable to offer you any form of compensation.

Thank you again for contacting us.

Yours sincerely

D Ayre

Dawn Ayre
Manager
Customer Relations

British Airways Plc
Registered Office: Waterside PO Box 365 Harmondsworth UB7 0GB
Registered in England No. 1777777

www.britishairways.com

"Cookeswithin"
99, Kerching Drive
Twickenham, Middx, UK.

Dawn Ayre
MANAGER Customer Relations
British Airways
PO Box 5619
Sudbury
Suffolk
CO10 2PG

15th July
Your Ref: 4198652

Dear Dawn,

Thank you for your letter in response to my letter sent to Kelly Robson. I am flattered that I have had a letter from you. However I wasn't asking for any compensation in my last letter although my first letter did include an Invoice for Taxis, which I was under the impression were included in my deal with British Airways.

May I suggest that I make for you a couple of "alternative" radio jingles (is that the correct name?) that would clarify this problem for any future passengers.

So when the words *"Including Taxes"* is said by the voice chap, I could add a **"KERCHING!"** sound, like a cash register. And then the voice could say *"What we don't mean is TAXIS!"*. And then I could add a **"VROOM, VROOM"**, sound effect like a car moving away from the curb. That would solve it yes? You'd certainly hear the difference then.

A close friend of one of my wife's teaching colleagues has a brother-in law who owns a small garden shed recording studio, and he's offered me a really good hourly rate. I have included this in the attached invoice so maybe we could split the costs? Do you think Saatchi's would be interested also?

I hope you don't mind my suggesting this, but I know that this could solve the problem once and for all. Please let me know. I'm excited not only to resolve this rather unfortunate issue for British Airways, but I've always fancied doing some recording in a studio. This could solve both in one swoop, so to speak.

Thank you again for taking the time to help with this problem, and I look forward to hearing from you in due course.

Kind Regards

Yours excitedly,

Bob Howard

Sales Invoice

Date: _____ Invoice No: _____

From: "Cookeswithin" 99, Kerching Drive, Twickenham, Middx, UK

Qty	Description	Amount exclusive of V.A.T. £	V.A.T. Net £
	Recording studio hourly rate as agreed by Trevor-sound, Twickenham	£35.00p	
	Estimated time to re-record one or two radio jingles. 4 hours	£140.00p	
	Sound effects disk hire, or internet download	£9.99p	
	Male voice to re-record the message for British Airways (special deal)	£50.00p	
	Total payable	£199.99p	
	50% charges to British Airways as agreed in letter	£99.99p	
		Sub total exc. V.A.T. £	
		V.A.T. £	
		Total due £	

V.A.T. rate............................
Payment terms........................
Tax Point ....

I'm sure if Saatchi and Saatchi are interested they could easily help with these costs.

Let me know if you think I should contact them directly.

BRITISH AIRWAYS

Customer Relations
PO Box 5619 (S506)
Sudbury Suffolk CO10 2PG UK
Tel 0870 850 9850
Tel +44 (0)191 490 7901
Fax +44 (0)20 8759 4314

22 July

Mr Bob Howard
Cookeswithin
99 Kerching Drive
Twickenham, Middx

Our Ref: 4198652

Dear Mr Howard

Thank you for your recent letter and the offer of making us some radio jingles.

I am sorry but our advertising is always planned for at least a year, as our agency has to work closely with marketing, brands and sales promotions throughout the world.

Once again thank you for your suggestions and taking the trouble to write to us.

Yours sincerely

D. Ayre

Dawn Ayre
Manager
Customer Relations

British Airways Plc
Registered Office Waterside PO Box 365 Harmondsworth UB7 0GB
Registered in England No. 1777777

www.britishairways.com

"Cookeswithin"
99, Kerching Drive
Twickenham, Middx, UK

Oxford English Dictionary
Oxford University Press
Great Clarendon St.
Oxford OX2 6DP

23rd November

Dear Sir,

I was wondering what it took to get a word accepted into the *Oxford English Dictionary*? I have quite a few that I would like you to consider and if possible add to the next edition, whenever that may be.

Hostulate. *verb.* To interrupt after a question has been asked. BBC Interviewers seem to *Hostulate* when requesting a speedy answer under pressure to a question. Using the phrase "To sum up in one word".

Very similar to:

Enprickle. *verb.* Hostility under pressure, especially in an interview.

Didogratory. *adverb* . Inability to sing in tune whilst creating exceptionally boring and repetitive melodies.

Hucknard. *noun.* One who sings painfully sharp.

Wubble. *noun.* Someone unable to pronounce the letter *"R"*. A fashion so it would appear with most personalities.

Excresentainer. *noun.* Someone totally lacking in talent.

And similar to: **Nabilitive.** *adverb.* Devoid of any ability. Sadly these two words describe most TV presenters, and B, C, D and E-Z list celebrities.

I would also like to find out what you know about **Fockule** and **Ouble**? Both excellent words.

I await with interest your reply and hopefully good news with respect to inclusion in the next edition of the Dictionary. I have attached an invoice for my new words. Once they're paid for they are yours!

Yours most sincerely

Bob Howard

Bob Howard

Sales Invoice

Invoice No: _____
Date: _____
From: _____

To: Cost and Ownership of the following words:

Qty	Description	Amount exclusive of V.A.T.P
	Hostulate.	£66.00p
	Enprickle	£39.99p
	Didogratory	£45.87p
	Hucknard	£67.00p
	Wubble	£32.88p
	Excresentainer	£78.78p
	Nabilitive,	£18.99p
	Total payable	£339.51p

OXFORD
UNIVERSITY PRESS

Academic Division
Managing Director: Tim Barton

Great Clarendon Street
Oxford OX2 6DP
United Kingdom

+44 (0) 1865 556767 *telephone*
+44 (0) 1865 556646 *fax*
www.oup.com

A/Ask Oxford/JEAF/mc

1 December

Dear Mr Howard,

Thank you for your letter of 23 November to the *Oxford English Dictionary*.

The answer to your initial question, 'What does it take to get a word accepted into the *Oxford English Dictionary*?' is chiefly concerned with usage and currency. We would not begin to consider researching into a word or sense that was not yet in the dictionary until we were able to find a substantial body of published evidence for its use. This evidence could be from any kind of published material, but would need to be from a range of different sources and authors, and would need to cover a timespan of at least ten years.

Once such evidence could be found, we would then be able to initiate research to enable us to build up as complete a picture as possible of the word's history and origin and current usage. At this stage it would still be possible for us to decide that there was not enough evidence to justify an entry in the *OED*, bearing in mind that once a word is included it cannot be removed.

I think you will see from this that the words you mention, enjoyable though they are, are likely to be too ephemeral or otherwise limited in their application to become a significant part of the language.

I am sorry that I can tell you nothing about the words 'fockule' and 'ouble', as they do not feature as words in any of our current resources, except that 'ouble' can be found accidentally isolated as part of longer words such as *double* and *trouble*.

I am sorry if you will find this response disappointing.

Yours sincerely,

Mrs J. E. A. Field
Senior Editor
Oxford English Dictionary

Oxford University Press is a department
of the University of Oxford. It furthers
the University's objective of excellence
in research, scholarship, and education
by publishing worldwide

"Cookeswithin"
99, Kerching Drive
Twickenham, Middx, UK

Ofcom Contact Centre,
Riverside House,
2a, Southwark Bridge Road,
London SE1 9HA.

8th April

Dear Sir or Madam,

I didn't really want to write to you. I wanted to write to GMTV but sadly I was unable to get their postal address, and felt a fax to them was too frivolous. Knowing that you specialise in matter of taste, decency and standards, however, I felt that you were a perfectly suitable second choice. My letter concerns the GMTV programme LK today, which is Lorraine Kelly today, in case you didn't already know.

Each morning, my TV alarm goes off at 8 am, and I am greeted by the day's news and weather, the, feisty Fiona Phillips, and homey "Chubby" Eamonn Holmes. So far so good. Then at 8.30, Lorraine Kelly appeared and I was aware of something very unpleasant happening. It was a feature on people getting married for the second time. Not only was this pointless, uninteresting non-event wasting valuable broadcast time, it was being hosted by a camp male presenter whose total knowledge of marriage would have been limited to a row of marquees, if you get my drift? It was unbelievably bad and meaningless, and as they started to discuss *"The first song they danced to at their wedding"* I awoke in a panic, to try to find the remote so I could turn the TV off.

This is where it gets silly.

I jumped out of bed, kicking the remote under the wardrobe at the far end of the room, and realising that I wouldn't be able to retrieve it quickly, I dived for the plug socket so I could end this TV misery once and for all. But on the way to the plug socket, I stood on the cable, and pulled the entire TV off its stand, causing the bowl of flowers that was on top of the TV to crash to the ground. There was an almighty explosion as the TV and vase collided, and steam started to pour from the back, filling my bedroom with grey smoke. Then the smoke alarm went off, and I had to remove the batteries to stop the noise.

I had managed to rid myself of Lorraine, the funny little marriage expert, and the couple on the sofa finally, but my TV and a perfectly good vase were no more.

So that's it really. A sad, unfortunate story I'm sure you would admit.

But I feel that I am justified in enclosing an invoice of costs for which I personally hold GMTV responsible, that include my TV, vase, and other related damaged goods caused directly by one of their programmes. If there is any way you could pass these on to GMTV, and Lorraine herself, I would be very grateful. I know that coming from you they would take some notice.

And in future, it would be great if they could stick to stories that wouldn't cause such distress as this one did, and think about the many viewers who are not completely alert and awake at that time in the morning.

I look forward to an amicable outcome to this request.

Yours most sincerely

Bob Howard
Bob Howard

Sales Invoice

Date: _____ Invoice No: _____

From: "Cookeswithin" 99, Kerching Drive, Twickenham, Middx, UK

Qty	Description	Amount exclusive of V.A.T. £	V.A.T. Net £
	Purchase of new TV, stand and remote		£650.00p
	New Vase		£ 12.99p
	Flowers		£ 15.89p
	Hook and arm contraption to retrieve remote from under wardrobe		£ 18.79p
	Batteries for smoke alarm		£ 6.72p
		Sub total exc. V.A.T.£	
		V.A.T.£	
		Total due £	£714.39p

V.A.T. rate: _____
Payment terms: _____
Tax Point: _____

Ref: 2429047

OFFICE OF COMMUNICATIONS

15 April

Mr B. Howard
"Cookeswithin"
99 Kerching Drive
Twickenham
Middx

Alistair Hall
Case Officer

Direct Line: 020 7783 4445
Direct Fax: 0845 456 3333

Dear Mr Howard

Thank you for your letter of 8 April.

We've noted your distaste at a recent item on GMTV and the unfortunate series of mishaps that occurred as a result of this.

We do investigate complaints about programme content, but this is more from the point of view of ensuring broadcasters do not cause widespread offence rather than pursuing individual claims for damages such as yours. Therefore any suggestion that GMTV should pay you damages should be pursued with them directly. If you have not contacted GMTV already their address is as follows (I return copies of your letter to us should this be of assistance):

GMTV Ltd
The London Television Centre
Upper Ground
London
SE1 9TT
Duty office 0870 243 4333 (6am-1pm)
Web site: www.gmtv.co.uk

Yours sincerely,

Alistair Hall

The London Television Centre Upper Ground London SE1 9TT
Telephone 020 7827 7000 Facsimile 020 7827 7001 www.gm.tv

Mr Bob Howard
Cookeswithin
99 Kerching Drive
Twickenham, Middx

3 August

Dear Mr Howard

Thank you very much for your letter of 20 May and many apologies for the delay in replying to you. In order to clear up one misconception that you mention in your letter, I would confirm that GMTV has a policy of replying to EVERY letter in due course, whether they are solicited or unsolicited.

With regard to the unfortunate circumstances that you found yourself in, after oversleeping on Wednesday 6 April, I'm afraid that it isn't possible for GMTV to admit any liability for the accident to your television set, vase, flowers, hook and arm contraption to retrieve remote from under wardrobe (whatever that might be!) and batteries for your smoke alarm. GMTV is watched by 6 million viewers a day and a good proportion of them tune in specifically for the LK Today segment of the show. As broadcasters, it would not be in our interest to transmit a programme that no-one wanted to watch.

However, we do accept that one man's meat is another man's poison and we are very sorry that, on this occasion, this meat was your poison. Hopefully, this is a situation that will not recur in the future.

Yours sincerely

Gay Phillips
Viewers' Correspondence Co-ordinator

GMTV Limited Registered in England No 2578005

www.ingramcontent.com/pod-product-compliance
Lightning Source LLC
Chambersburg PA
CBHW032121090426
42743CB00007B/419